Apostle of the Highlands
An Illustrated Abridgement

The Life of St. Columba, the Apostle and Patron of the
Ancient Scots and Picts and Joint Patron of the Irish

Marjorie Kunch
Foreword by V. Rev. Archpriest Mark A. Rowe

PASCHA PRESS
Educate   Edify   Entertain

Copyright 2019 Marjorie Kunch

All rights reserved. No part of the edited publication or its illustrations may be reproduced or transmitted in any form or by any means electronic or mechanical, including photocopy, recording, or any storage and retrieval system now known or to be invented without prior written permission from the publisher or author.

Pascha Press

Toll-free telephone: 1-844-4-PASCHA mkunch@paschapress.com
http://www.paschapress.com

This publication is designed to provide accurate information, for general purposes only, in regard to the subject matter covered. There are no warranties, expressed or implied.

ISBN: 978-0-9964045-7-0

Dedication

In honor of my maternal ancestors: the Burtons-of Welsh and English stock, and to the Websters-a sept of the MacFarlane clan who originated from Aberdeen, Scotland. They left the Isles, headed for America by way of Canada, to ultimately settle in Northwest Indiana for coveted steel mill jobs. A nod to my uncle Louis Greer, himself of proud Irish ancestry, who sparked my interest in all things Celtic at an early age through his gifts of storytelling and art; and who inspired me to likewise travel abroad to my ancestral homeland. Lastly, it is also to the priests, monks, nuns, and parishioners of Scotland who toil in one of Orthodoxy's westernmost European vineyards that I dedicate this translation. Thank you for all you do to Glorify Him!

> *Never, never, never let anyone tell you that, in order to be Orthodox, you must be Eastern. The West was fully Orthodox for a thousand years, and her venerable liturgy is far older than any of her heresies.*
>
> *-St. John Maximovitch*

By the hand of Aidan Hart

Credits

Book designer and cover artist: Scott Cuzzo, www.scottcuzzo.com

Cover: St. Martin Cross, Iona. Also known as "Hy, the Land of Ravens"

St. Columba Iconography:
Courtesy of Aidan Hart, www.aidanharticons.com

Images: Marjorie Kunch – Shot on location in the Hebrides, Scotland, UK

Timeline information: www.wikipedia.org

Original materials sourced from the public domain. Abridged, compiled, edited, and illustrated so as to be more easily understandable for a modern audience.

Source: The Life of St. Columba, the Apostle and Patron Saint of the Ancient Scots and Picts, and Joint Patron of the Irish; Commonly Called Columkille, the Apostle of the Highlands-By John Smith, One of the Ministers of Campbelton; Honorary Member of the Antiquarian and Highland Societies of Scotland.

Originally published by Mundell & Son, and J. Mundell, College, Glasgow, 1798

Note from The Publisher

This project stems from my deep love for the saints of my ancestral homeland. Thanks be to God, I was lead to Orthodoxy in 2005 from the heathen background of my teenage years. Imagine my surprise to learn the ancient Celtic lands were Orthodox fully one thousand years prior to the Slavic countries that typically comes to mind! Following a calling I have had since childhood to travel overseas, I set foot in my beloved United Kingdom for the first time in June of 2016. It was humbling to have walked the very same Ionian sands St. Columba walked. I had also participated in the first Divine Liturgy served on St. Brendan's monastic isle, Eileach an Naoimh, in nearly a millennia. This tiny rock, part of the Garvellachs in the Firth of Lorne, is believed to have been settled by Orthodox monks in 542 AD. St. Columba frequented the island and viewed it as a retreat from the demands of Iona. Best known for having unique beehive cell ruins, it is thought that the original early monastic buildings were destroyed by Norse invaders in the 7th century and were later rebuilt by disciples from Iona in the 9th century. Standing in their presence, these stones seem to still ring out the song of prayer by the brave monastics. This isle is also where the mother of St. Columba, Eithne, is buried; and it is where we celebrated a Panakhida for her. It was during this serendipitous pilgrimage that the seeds for creating a series about Scottish Orthodox saints took root, and in your hands is the first fruit of my labors.

First published in 1798 by Mundell & Son of Glasgow, I have updated this work by removing the peculiarities of the printed word in 18th century Britain, "f" in place of "s" for example, so as to be easily legible for a modern audience. I also minimally edited some of the original language and syntax, while always keeping an eye on retaining the charm of John Smith's prose. I integrated and abridged select footnotes, interesting yet copious when left in their entirety, into the body of work where appropriate and included some modern photographs I had taken of the lands mentioned in this historic text. I have also interwoven a fascinating comparison of world events into the timeline of the history on Iona in the appendix. May the knowledge from centuries ago shared in these pages bloom within your heart. Glory be to Jesus Christ, glory be forever!

-Marjorie Kunch, Pascha Press

Foreword

It is a wonderful and undeserved honor to be asked to provide a brief foreword to this book detailing the life and ministry of our venerable and God-Bearing Father Columba of Iona, Enlightener of Scotland. The stories and chronicles of the ministry and miracles of Saint Columba during his earthly life are inspiring as well as aid the reader in a deeper sense of Orthodox spirituality.

This work, which has been translated and abridged from the original, provides a clear and reader-friendly journey into the life of our Holy Father Columba. Saint Columba is also sometimes referred to as 'Columcille', which means 'dove of the Church.' There is no doubt that his life and ministry was a gift from God to the Isles where he was called. The spirituality of Iona is nothing short of legendary, and the book asserts that no less that 100 of Saint Columba's scholars or disciples were glorifed as Saints. The fruits of his holy ministry are evident in the life of the Holy Church, and continue to bless the faithful.

It is truly fitting that this remastered work should come while we are indeed amid a new resurgence of Western Orthodoxy. These holy treasures are incredibly valuable to us as we struggle along in our own spiritual journey. We can acquire a real sense of the 'phronema' or mindset of our Holy Father Columba, and learn to apply his insights and teachings to our continued goal of being as close to Christ as we can in this life, and therefore be able to spend eternity with Him in the next.

> *O God! Who didst our Father hear,*
> *Be to his children ever near;*
> *And grace vouchsafe to lead us on,*
> *Until we meet him at thy throne.*
> *(Translation of a stanza of a Hymn used in the Feast of St Columba)*

Saint Columba, pray to God for us.

With every blessing,

The Very Reverend Archpriest Mark A. Rowe
Vicar General, ROCOR Western Rite Communities

Iona from the sea

Preface

There is implanted in the mind of a person a principle of curiosity, which makes him or her desirous of knowing the manners and customs of others in different places and in former times. This desire is particularly strong in regard to what relates to one's own country. We then feel a more than ordinary interest in viewing those customs, manners, and modes of thinking and acting, which prevailed in the days of our forefathers.

To satisfy this curiosity, no mean is so likely as the particular history, anecdotes, and memoires of the people who, in their time, made the greatest figure in their country. In this view, the following account of St. Columba may not, perhaps, be unworthy of the perusal of such who wish to know something of the state of religion and society in the Highlands about twelve (now fifteen-editor) hundred years ago.

No man ever lived to whom the Highlands and Isles of Scotland were more indebted to than St. Columba; and, perhaps, few lived to whom the British Isles in general were under stronger obligations. It was Columba who kindled that torch, which, in the darkest ages, shed its kindly rays far beyond the limits of the Highlands, and which contributed much to enlighten even the south of Britain. According to the testimony of the venerable Bede, England was indebted, as many of its most learned and pious divines came to the seminary of learning established by Columba in a remote and obscure corner of the Highlands. Such are the revolutions effected by Time in this world of strange vicissitudes!

In a period in which biography is so much in vogue, an account of the life of so extraordinary a man, and of such a benefactor to his country and to mankind, may claim some little attention from those who may perhaps at this day be in part indebted for their comforts to the fruits of his labor and instructions. The conqueror of kingdoms may claim our admiration, but the enlightener and civilizer of nations deserves our love, esteem, and respect. The memory of the one, without any imputation of ingratitude, may be suffered to perish; but the memory of the other deserves to be honored.

The general task at present is for books of a light, cheerful, and amusing cast. But why may not even the readers of such books diversify their amusement, and bestow an hour or two on the perusal of the history of a man, who may now be considered as so singular and extraordinary a character, that his life may well pass for novel? If, in the midst of gaiety, this should for a moment dispose them to be serious, where would be the great harm? Or, should it lead them to reflect for a little on the power of religion, with its pleasures and prospects, as exhibited in the life of Columba, what reason can they have to think that they should afterwards repent it; or that the time was not well bestowed? Among the many expedients which they use for passing the time, might they not try, for once, see how the reading an account of the life of a saint would pass a little of it?

To the man who is truly pious and religious, the life of Columba cannot fail to be entertaining and useful. It will show him the power of Divine grace upon the soul, and the progress that may be made in holiness by a man entirely devoted to God. Aspiring to as high a degree as possible of glory, honor, and immortality. The contemplation of such a life will attract his regard, and powerfully engage him, in part at least, to follow the example.

But the life of St. Columba is calculated to be still more useful to those in holy orders; as it furnishes them with a lively example of fidelity and zeal in the discharge of their important office, and with a fair copy of every grace and virtue that should adorn the sacred character. To examine how other men in the same profession have discharged the duty to which we are called, what manner of men they have been, and what manner of works they have done. This may lead us to consider what we ourselves are, and how we ought to act, so as to obtain the WELL-DONE of our Lord, when we shall be called to give an account of our stewardship.

A laudable spirit for propagating the gospel in foreign parts is, as present, gone abroad. To the missionaries employed in this important work, it may be useful to have the example of a man who devoted his life to the same business. To know the means which he used, and the manner in which he acted, so as to have attained such wonderful successes. For few, if any since the days of the Apostles, had more success in preaching the gospel to the heathens than the venerable St. Columba. May God, for Christ's sake, endow all who are engaged in the same office with a portion of the same spirit!

Reilig Odhrain, St. Oran's Cemetery, Iona. A burial ground in use during St. Columba's time. The resting place of Irish, Norse, and Scottish kings, including the storied Macbeth

The Life Of St. Columba

The life of St. Columba (called Columbanus by the venerable Bede, and in the language of his country called Colum-cille, or Colum of the Cells, for having founded so many churches and monasteries), the Apostle of the Highlands and Western Isles of Scotland, and the founder and first abbot of the famous monastery of Iona, was written by two of his successors, Cummin and Adomnan. The former of these wrote about sixty, and the latter about eighty-three years after the death of the saint; so that they had very good opportunities of coming at the knowledge of every part of his life and character.

But, unhappily, it seems not to have been the object of those good men to delineate the real life and character of the saint but rather to give a marvelous detail of visions, prophecies, and miracles which they boldly ascribe to him. It is candid to suppose that they themselves believed what they wrote, and that their writings may have been of use in those ages of credulity and fable. Although in our more enlightened times, they rather disgust than edify in that antiquated form. It is therefore necessary, if we would peruse the life of this great and holy man with patience and with profit, to strip it of that marvelous garb with which it has been so long invested, to separate the fact from the fable, and to show the saint in his real character.

In attempting this, I shall make no further use of that mass of wonders which I mentioned, than as it serves to illustrate the character of Columba or the spirit of the times in which he lived. Of those marvelous relations I do not profess to believe any, nor would I be so bold as to deny them all. In circumstances such as those in which Columba stood, called forth to extirpate an old and inveterate superstition, and to establish the true religion upon its ruins, to surmount the prejudices of a barbarous people, and to contend with powerful and artful priests, we cannot, without presumption, say how far it might be fit that God should countenance the labors of His faithful servant, and vouchsafe him even by signs and wonders, as He often did to his ministers in such cases, a clear and decided victory. A reflection somewhat similar to this is made by one of his biographers, after mentioning the issue of a contest to which the saint was challenged by the Pictish priests or druids, before an immense crowd of spectators near the royal palace at Loch Ness.

But of these matters, as we must allow ourselves to be very incompetent judges, it is our wisdom to be silent. The life of Columba is abundantly uncommon and interfering without them; and his example, as it will in that case be the more imitable, will be also the more useful. A view to imitation in usefulness only do I attempt to unfold this holy man's life and character.

Columba was a native of Ireland, descended from the royal family of that kingdom and nearly allied to the kings of Scotland. His father was Felim, the son of Fergus, who was grandson of the great Nial the King of Ireland. The wife (corrected from mother-editor) of Felim was Eithne of Leinster, daughter of Lorn, who first reigned in conjunction with his brother Fergus, over the Scots or Dalreudini in Argyllshire. Like many others who made a conspicuous figure in the world, his birth is said to have been preceded by some extraordinary circumstances. Maveth, the disciple of St. Patrick, is said to have predicted the birth and name of Columba, and the lasting glory which he should acquire by converting the Western Isles to Christianity.

His mother, also when pregnant with the saint, dreamed one night that a person, whose figure and mien seemed to denote him to be more than human (angelic), had presented her with a veil or garment of the most beautiful texture and colors; that in a little time, however, he resumed his gift, and raising and expanding it in the sky, allowed it to fly through heaven. As it flew, it continued to extend itself on all hands, over mountains and plains, till at length it covered an expanse which her eye was not able to measure. Finding what she had once possessed thus gone out of her reach, and likely to be irrecoverably lost, she could not help expressing her sorrow and regret, till the angel thus addressed her, "Be not grieved at not being allowed to retain this valuable gift but for a very short time. It is an emblem of that child of which thou art soon to be the mother, for him hath God ordained, as one of his prophets, to be extensively useful upon earth, and to lead an innumerable company of souls to heaven."

Columba was born in the year 521, and his parents being thus, as they believed, admonished of the part which their son was destined to act in life, and to which they soon perceived his genius and early disposition to piety to be peculiarly adapted, lost no time in providing him with such education as tended to qualify him for the sacred office. They first put him under the care of Cruinechan, a devout presbyter, who discovered, as he thought, in his disciple while yet a child, extraordinary symptoms of his future glory and greatness.

Sometime after he studied under St. Finnian the Bishop of Clonard, a man of considerable learning who was so much charmed with the piety of Columba, that though he was yet but a youth, he used to give him the appellation of "Saint" and believed, from his uniformly holy and regular life, that he had obtained from God an angel from heaven to be his companion and guardian.

Fenbar, also a bishop and saint, is mentioned as one of Columba's masters. He too used to give his pupil the name of "Saint" and notwithstanding the great disparity of their years, seems to have treated him rather as a companion and friend than as a scholar, sometimes asking his opinion about the most dark and mysterious

Two photos of the resting place of St. Eithne, mother of St. Columba, on the isle of Eileach an Naoimh, also called Hinba. She retired here along with St. Columba's uncle, Ernan, prior of the monastery on Hinba founded by St. Brendan

dispensations of Providence. Under him the piety of Columba, now in deacon's orders, became so distinguished, that his fame was already spread over a great part of the kingdom, to which the following incident seems to have contributed not a little. One day as the old man read his book in the fields, a young girl, pursued by a barbarian, fled to him for protection. He immediately cried to his pupil, who

was reading at a little distance. The aid of both was unavailing; the ruffian, with one thrust of his spear, left her dead at their feet. "Ah!" said Gemman, "How long will God, the righteous Judge, allow this atrocious deed to go unpunished?"

"The soul of the murderer," replied Columba, "may yet be in hell as soon as that of the murdered in heaven." At that instant they observed the unhappy man fall dead at some distance. A sacrifice, it is probable, to the violence of his own passions, though ascribed by the people to the appeal which was made to heaven by Gemman and Columba.

Our saint spent also some time under St. Ciaran, who preached to the Attacotti or Dalreudini of Kintyre, +594. From him the parish of Kil-chiaran, of late called Campbelton, takes its name. He was the father and founder of the monastery of Clon, upon the Shenan. For this man, so venerable for his piety and zeal in preaching gospel, Columba retained always the strongest affection, and wrote a sacred ode upon his death, in which he celebrates his virtues.

How much Columba was loved and revered by his companions, during his stay in this place, appears from the wonderful veneration with which he was received when he came to visit them some time afterwards. All the people in the monastery and its neighborhood poured out to meet him, kissed him with the utmost reverence and affection, and singing hymns and psalms of praise, led him to their church, surrounded with a rail of wood, carried by four men, to prevent his being incommoded by so immense a multitude.

Whether he remained in the monastery at Clon till the death of Ciarnan is not mentioned; but in the succeeding year, the 28th of his age, we are told that he founded the monastery of Darmagh or Durrough, where a copy of the four Evangelists, which he had transcribed, was extant, in the last century, when Sir James Ware wrote his history.

It was probably in this interval, betwixt founding this monastery and coming to Britain, that Columba visited several foreign countries in which his piety, learning, and other accomplishments procured him the highest regard and esteem. From some of the eastern churches he is said to have borrowed the model of his monastic rule. In Italy he is said to have founded a monastery, and in France he was solicited

Eileach an Naoimh, formerly called Hinba

by King Sigibert, who made him large promises to remain with him. But Columba, whose ambition was to be useful rather than great, told him that he was so far from coveting the wealth of others that, for Christ's sake, he had already renounced his own.

How much time Columba spent in traveling, or when he returned home, we cannot say. Indeed, the chronological notices in the memoirs of his life which are left to us, are so few as to preclude every attempt at a regular series of history. We have, however, abundant materials for developing his life and character and this is what we have already professed to be our object.

View from the top of Hinba

Ireland had now for a long time enjoyed the light of the Gospel and abounded in saints and learned men, while the isles and northern parts of Scotland were still covered with darkness and in the shackles of superstition. On those dismal regions, therefore, Columba looked with a pitying eye, and, however forbidding the prospect resolved to become the Apostle of the Highlands. Accordingly, in the year 563, he set out in a wicker boat covered with hides, accompanied by twelve of his friends and followers, and landed in the Isle of Hi or Iona, near the confines of the Scottish and Pictish territories. This was the origin of the order of the Culdees in Scotland; an order of which Columba was the founder. He and his followers were distinguished for learning, purity of faith, and sanctity of life. Bede, in what he meant as a censure, commends them highly when he says, "They preached only such works of charity and piety as they could learn from the prophetical, evangelical, and apostolic writings. They firmly opposed the errors and superstitions of the Church of Rome, till towards the end of the 12th century, when they were at length overpowered and supplanted by a new race of monks, as inferior to them in learning and piety, as they surpassed them in wealth and ceremonies." per Ledwich's account. This place Columba probably chose, as being conveniently situated for his attending to the important concerns which he had to manage in Ireland, as well as for carrying on the work which he had in view in Scotland. Besides, if he should succeed in procuring a grant of it, he might discover in it those properties which were generally sought for in the site of religious houses.

Columba was now in the 42nd year of his age, and needed all his vigor of mind and body in encountering those difficulties, which presented themselves when he undertook the conversion of the northern Picts to Christianity. The nation was in so barbarous a state that some of them, regardless of the sanctity of his character, made more than once an attempt at his life. Once, in the dead of night, the village in which he slept was set alight. Another time, in the Isle of Hinba, a ruffian rushed upon him with his spear which one of his disciples, by the name of Finduchnan, stepped between to save his master and received the spear into his own bosom. His life was spared only by the thickness of his cuculla, or leather jacket. Once a king, not more civilized than his people, ordered his gate to be shut when the holy man first approached it. The priests or druids, too, as they held a vested interested, were most forward in opposing him, and wanted neither eloquence, influence, or art to effect their purpose. The country itself was wild, woody, and mountainous, and greatly infested with wild beasts, from which the life of the saint seems to have been more than once in imminent danger. And, what appears to have been the greatest difficulty of all, he was so little master of the dialect of that people, at least of some among them, or for the first while, as to need an interpreter when he preached to them the words of salvation.

The sign reads: "You stand amid the ruins of the most complete early Christian monastery in Scotland. It may have been founded by St. Brendan the Navigator in the mid-6th century, before St. Columba reached Iona. The earliest remains include: The inner enclosure, the monastery's heart. An underground cell for storage, punishment, or possibly a ritual 'purgatory.' A square base, possibly for a stone cross. A burial ground with a cross-marked gravestone. Far to your left is Eithne's grave, reputedly where St. Columba's mother is buried, while well-preserved double beehive cells are away to your right. Irish missionaries probably chose this island for their monastery as both an isolated sanctuary where they could lead perfect Christian lives and a well-connected base from which they could reach out to the people of what is now Scotland. Eileach an Naoimh seems to have been abandoned by the 9th century, when Viking raids devastated monasteries along Scotland's west coast. It may have been a place of pilgrimage in the 11th and 12th centuries, when the stone chapel was probably built, perhaps over an earlier chapel. A late medieval church is to the left. The farm buildings that reused much of the monastery's stonework were in use until the 1800s. The site remains unexcavated. Early Christian monks from across the British Isles had a different way of calculating Easter from the Roman Church. They also had a distinctive ear to ear monastic tonsure or haircut, shown in the 7th century Book of Durrow. Rome's rules on both were adopted in the 8th century."

Besides all this the austerity of his own manner, sometimes fasting for whole days, and watching and praying for whole nights, submitting to constant fatigue of body and anxiety of mind abroad, or the most intense application to study at home and withal so self-denied and crucified to the world, as to reject what we are now accustomed to consider as its innocent comforts and enjoyments. These were, all of them, circumstances very unfavorable in appearance to his making

The supposed stone pillow of St. Columba on display at the Iona Abbey museum

many proselytes. For example, at the age of 76, Columba's bed was the bare ground and his pillow was a stone. This very stone is said to reside in the great cathedral which stands on Iona today. And, we may add, that the strictest of his monastic rule, which imposed heavy spiritual tolls, enforced by the sanction of bodily chastisements, would also seem an unsurmountable bar to his gaining many disciples to his cloisters.

Notwithstanding all this, however, the labors of Columba were attended with a very astonishing degree of successes. In the course of a few years, the greater part of the Pictish kingdom was converted to the Christian faith. Monasteries were erected in many places and churches everywhere established with Columba, as Primate of all Irish churches per the council of Drimceat. This extended jurisdiction over all ecclesiastics of the Highlands and Isles; and monasteries of Dunkeld, Abernethy, Kilrimont aka St. Andrews, among others. He superintended and directed all the affairs of the Pictish and much of the Scottish and Irish churches, and was highly reverenced not only by the king of the Picts, but also by all neighboring princes who courted his acquaintance and liberally assisted him in his expensive undertakings. Wherever he visited abroad he was received with the highest demonstration both of respect and joy: crowds attended him on the road and to the place where he lodged at night, the neighborhood sent stores of provisions to entertain him, and when the multiplicity of his business allowed him to stay at home he was resorted to for aid and advice as a physician both of soul and body, by multitudes of every rank and denomination. Even the place of his residence was considered peculiarly holy and to sleep in the dust of it became, for ages, an object of ambition to kings and princes. According to tradition, forty-eight kings of Scotland, four of Ireland, and eight of Norway are buried at Iona. His monastery was the chief seminary of learning at the time, perhaps in Europe, and the nursery from which not only all the monasteries and above 300 churches which he himself has established, but also many of those in neighboring nations were supplied with learned divines and able pastors.

How then are we to account for this great and rapid successes of Columba, for there is no certainty of his having been endowed either with the gift of prophecy or with the power of working miracles? No doubt the Providence of God smiled upon his labors and perhaps we might discover a coincidence of favorable circumstances in the history of the times. But we are more concerned to seek for the cause in the character and conduct of the man, by which he was rendered so eminently qualified for the sacred office, and so successful, under God, in the discharge of it. The investigation of this subject is deserving of the attention of ministers, and not unworthy of the curiosity of all people.

That Columba's talents were of a very superior kind is not to be doubted. An uncommon greatness of soul is marked in every part of his extensive schemes, and the happy execution and successes of them are pregnant proofs of wisdom, perseverance, zeal, and abilities.

Firmness and fortitude are no less conspicuous in Columba's character. When he came to Britain, he seems to have been well aware of the difficulty of his undertaking, and of the time and toil which it should cost him to accomplish it. But instead of shrinking back, he only prayed to God to give him thirty years of life, which he devoted to his service, hoping that by the aid of divine grace he should in that period accomplish his designs.

We must also allow Columba a very extraordinary share of address, personal accomplishments, and colloquial talents, when he could so effectually recommend himself wherever he went, although a perfect stranger, as to be soon respected, loved, and cherished. How he could gain such ascendency over so many princes, as to be revered and patronized by all of them, when all of them were in a state of barbarism and seldom at peace among themselves is a sure proof this: that his conduct was always guarded with the utmost caution and prudence, that he never stepped out of his own line, nor did he take any concern whatever in state affairs when he could by any means avoid it. Once, indeed, he put the crown on the head of King Aidan, but he seems to have done it with reluctance, and pleads the strong necessity of having been compelled to it by a supernatural agent.

The same prudence and address may be discovered in his having been able to maintain good discipline, order, and subordination in so many monasteries, and so remote from one another. He directs the religious affairs of a great part of several nations, differing considerably in language and customs, superintends the education of youth, furnishes so many churches with fit pastors, and to do all this in such a manner that the growing love and veneration of men seem to have invariably kept pace with his years. To which we may add, that his sagacity in discovering probable effects from known causes, may have probably acquired him the reputation of being a prophet. To these talents, which were accompanied with the most engaging address and a pleasant cheerful countenance, was joined another very essential property in a preacher: a most powerful and commanding voice, which Adomnan says he could on occasion raise so as to resemble peals of thunder, and make it to be distinctly heard at a mile's distance when he chanted psalms.

That these natural endowments of Columba were highly cultivated by the best education and learning which the times could afford is clear from the mention already made of so many of his masters. A particular account of his studies, indeed, is not transmitted to us, but they seem by no means to have been confined to that profession which he followed but to have extended much further into the general circle of science. For his knowledge of physic, or skill in healing diseases, was so great that his cures were often considered as miracles. In some of Columba's cures, supposed by Adomnan to be miraculous, mention is made of his sprinkling the diseased person or beast with water, in which a cake or medicament had been infused, and of his making use of water into which he had put some stone or fossil. From this probably sprung some superstitious practices, not yet quite extinct in the Highlands, where many families have some pebble or crystal and sprinkle diseased cattle with the water in which it has been immersed. Columba's medicine is lost, and only the form of administering it is retained. And in the history, laws, and customs of different nations, he was so well versed, that he made a principal figure in the great council held at Drimceat, about the right of succession to the Scottish throne.

But whatever degree of knowledge and education Columba might have received in his earlier years, he never ceased, by intense study and application, to add to it. Every moment which so active and pious a life could spare from its main business, was devoted to study. Sometimes he heard his disciples read, and sometimes he read himself; sometimes he transcribed, and sometimes read what had been transcribed by others. It was by thus teaching the use of letters, and establishing a seminary of learning, that Columba did the greatest service to his country. He thus kindled a light which shone in a dark place for many generations, and by its kindly beams cherished the seed which he had sowed and brought it forward to an abundant harvest. Without this, all his personal virtues and personal labors could have produced but a comparatively small and temporary effect. In his life, we find mention made occasionally of various books of his writing and copying. As he wished his usefulness to man to be commensurate with the moments of his life and to make a part of the ultimate preparation for heaven, he spent some time in transcribing the Psalter, even on that very night on which he knew and told he was to be translated to eternal day.

In the character of Columba, talents, learning, and a constant application to study, make a very conspicuous figure. Still a more striking part of it is an early, uniform, and strong spirit of piety. Devoted from his birth to the service of God, and ardently bent on the pursuit of holiness, he seems to have almost reached the goal before others think of starting in the race. The appellation of saint was given him, as we have already seen, while he was yet a child. But far from resting in any measure of sanctity acquired in early life, he incessantly labored after higher and higher degrees of it to his latest day. In every moment, in every motion, and in every action of his life, he seems to have maintained upon his spirit a lively sense, a strong impression, and almost a clear vision of the presence of God. And surely a saint, without being accounted a visionary, may be allowed to see with the eyes of the mind and by the light of divine truth, the preference of spiritual essences, with as clear and satisfying a conviction of their reality as that which he has of outward objects in open day. Such seems to have been the case with Columba and therefore we need not wonder, if in everything small and great, he had so constant a regard to God.

"When do you purpose to sail, Columba?" said the magician or druid Broichan.

"On the third day hence," replied the saint, "if it be the will of God, and that I am then alive."

Broichan says, "You cannot, for I will raise contrary winds, and spread over you mists and darkness."

To which the saint answers, "All things are under the control of the Omnipotent God, and every motion of mine is undertaken in His name, and entirely guided by his direction."

In every affair of lesser moment, Columba shows the same regard to God and the same spirit of piety. If he only ascended his little car, when a car became necessary, he implored upon it the benediction of Him who only could give it power to carry, and whose providence could keep it from falling. If the milk from the fold passed him every day, every day it had his solemn benediction. If he looked on the corn by which his family was to be fed, he could not fail of saying, "Blessed be God!" or "God bless it!" If the wind blew this way or that, he took occasion from it either to pray to God, or to thank Him, with an eye to his friends as the course of it concerned. If he visited a pious friend, the first salutations were mixed with alleluia, and the soul had its spiritual entertainment before the body was yet received.

"Saint Columba, or Columkil," says the author of *The Life of Kentigern*, "left his island of Yi, to see the saint of Glasgow. When he approached the monastery, all went forth with sacred songs to meet him while he and his party also came forward, singing their melodious alleluias. And after the godly men had met, abundance of spiritual entertainment preceded their bodily refreshment." Perhaps some, who judge only by the manners of modern times, may suppose some ostentation is mixed with piety. But the manners even of saints, taking a tincture from the times, are very different now from what they were then, and piety, even where it may be genuine and true, is much less fervent. In those primitive and pious times, if two good men walked together on the road, they could solace themselves under the fatigues of their journey by singing the Psalms of David, and refresh themselves when they sat down by reading a portion of the Scriptures. If they did so now, they would be rated as wrong-headed enthusiasts, or charged with ostentation and perhaps hypocrisy. Columba's piety, however, was so far from being ostentatious that its luster was nowhere so conspicuous as in retirement and solitude. Hence the strong desire of some of his disciples to find an opportunity of being sometimes the secret witness of the earnestness, or rather ecstasy, of their master's private devotion. And from the accounts which they give us of what they saw and heard, we cannot greatly blame their curiosity.

True, these accounts have somewhat of a miraculous air in the relation of Cumin and Adomnan, and perhaps they ought to be received with some grains of allowance. Yet it is not for us to say, whether a man of such exalted piety and of so heavenly a frame of mind, under labors which needed uncommon support and consolation, might not, on some special occasions, enjoyed a higher degree of communion with God. A stronger manifestations of His favor than falls within the experience, or perhaps belief, of ordinary Christians. In these accounts we find frequent mention of a heavenly light seen at times to shine around him while engaged in devotion. This is so foreign to our experience that we might find it easier to doubt or deny the truth of the fact, than to give a satisfying account of it. But in things

The tomb of St. Kentigern, also known as St. Mungo

that are too high for us, modesty becomes us. We know that such appearances were familiar to other holy men, when those angels who were their ministering spirits did, for wise and gracious purposes, manifest their presence. This, when the angel who instructed Daniel manifested himself, was as the appearance of lightening. When the angel appeared to Peter, a light shone in the prison, and when our Savior, after His ascension, manifested His presence to Saul on the

The interior of St. Kentigern's Cathedral, Glasgow

way to Damascus and to John in Patmos, a heavenly glory shone around with so much brightness that mortal eyes could not endure its splendor. It is not for us to limit the Holy One of Israel and say when,

*The exterior of the Glasgow Cathedral where
St. Kentigern is entombed*

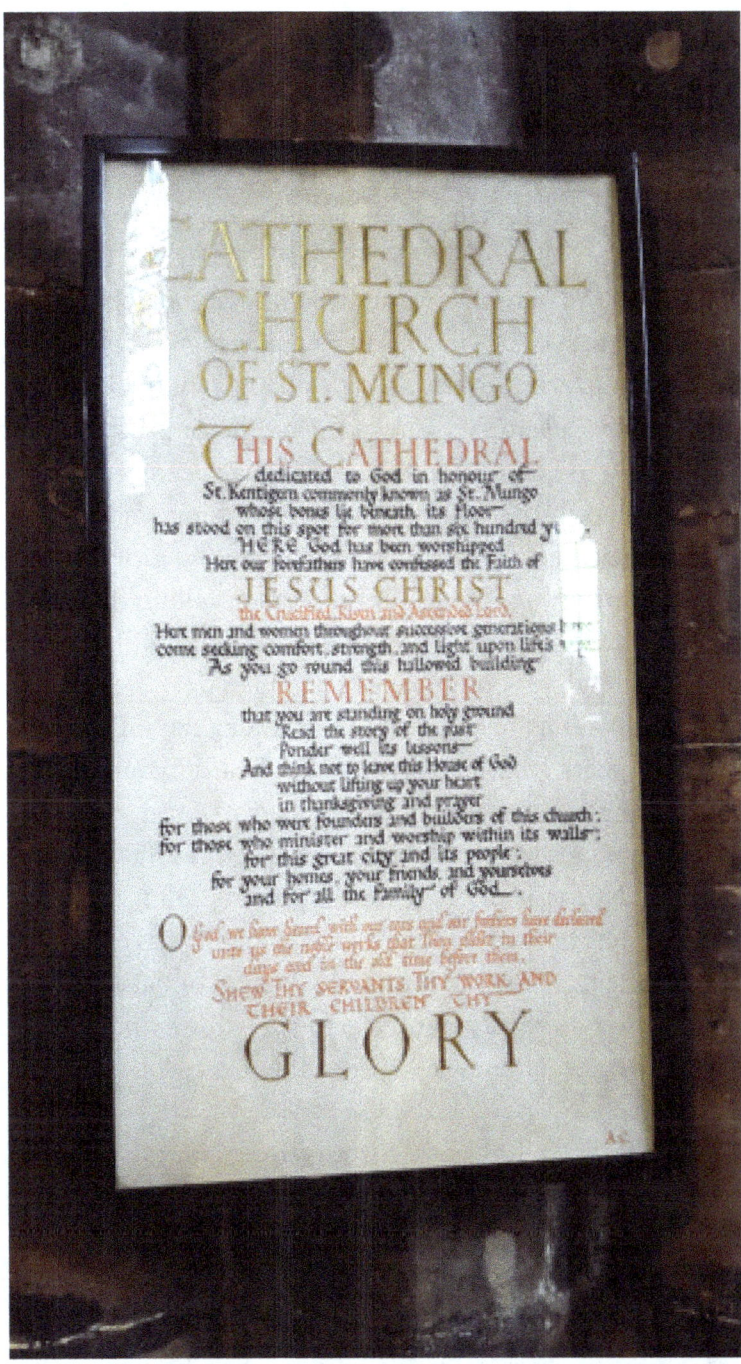

Plaquard found within the Cathedral of St. Kentigern

or when not, such manifestations were necessary or proper. It is not for us to say whether God might not favor such a man as Columba, and in such circumstances with some extraordinary manifestations of His presence, and with some sensible manifestations of the presence and society of celestial beings.

It may be observed here that Columba addresses angels in a style the very reverse of prayer or invocation, considering them only as fellow servants or ministering spirits. "I bade an angel of the Lord, who just now stood among us, to save one of the brethren just falling from the top of a high house, and how amazing is the speed of angels! Quick as lightning, and in the twinkling of an eye the angel reached him, though at a great distance, before he reached the ground, and saved him from suffering the smallest hurt." A man falling from the top of a very high house and not hurt, was no bad proof of the miraculous interposition to which Columba ascribed his safety. Be this as it may, he himself, as well as his disciples, was under the influence of such a belief, as appears from his having been heard (when not aware of it) as addressing his speech to attendant spirits. And it is certain that this belief would greatly contribute to enliven his piety and animate his devotion. Nor is it improbable that it was founded in reality, if we consider that he was so far from wishing to have these matters published that under the sanctions of a solemn or oath he commonly charged the few who accidently came to know, that they, in his lifetime at least, should never speak of them.

Of Columba's piety, however, a more unequivocal proof was his having lived a life of prayer and of praise. He was so attentive to morning and evening prayers that he seems never to have allowed himself to dispense with the performance of them, in any place, or on any pretense whatever. Thus, in the midst of infidels, enemies, scoffers, and disturbers of his devotion, when he had no house to cover him, we find him keep up his custom of glorifying God by stated and public worship. When at home this service was performed by him in the church, where we find him punctually attending, even on the last day of his life.

Father Seraphim Aldea celebrating the first Divine Liturgy in nearly a millennia on Eileach an Naoimh, known as Hinba in St. Columba's day. It was no small undertaking for the pilgrims to navigate the sea cliffs whilst carrying the necessary liturgical items to this uninhabited and wild place

Besides these public prayers, the monastic rule of Columba enjoined other very considerable exercises. He required the monks to, "Assemble thrice every night, and as often in the day. In every office of the day, they were to use prayers and sing three psalms. In the offices of the night, from October to February, they were to sing thirty-six psalms and twelve anthems at three several times: through the rest of the year, twenty-one psalms and eight anthems; but on Saturday and Sabbath nights, twenty-five psalms and as many anthems." And all this the saint himself performed with such alacrity that he was the first to enter the church to midnight vigils on the very night he died.

Of Columba's private prayers no particular account can be expected. But from the frequent mention which is made of his praying in his closet, and in his little oratory, and of his retiring frequently in the daytime to solitary places remote from the tumult and interruption of men, and of his going to the church or some retired place in the nighttime while others slept, we see that his life and soul was in this holy exercise. So much so indeed that, though at times his private prayers were not prolix, yet when in places in which he could attend to prayer and contemplation without being interrupted, we find him sometimes continuing in it for whole nights and days without either eating or drinking. A fast of three days, upon extraordinary and important occasions, was not in those times uncommon. In the austerity of life, some of Columba's followers seem to have exceeded their master and fasting (then thought an excellent mean of bringing the body into subjection to the soul, or of "taming the beast by stinting him of his food") though now gone out of fashion, was always one of the marks in their character. It is remarkable that most of these saints lived to extreme old age, Columba to his 96th year, many lived to 100, and St. Patrick to 120.

It seems also to have been his invariable rule to undertake no work, nor engage in any business, without having first invoked God. If about to officiate in any ministerial duty, he would first implore the Divine Presence to aid and enable him to discharge it properly. If he himself, or any of his friends, were to go any whither, by sea or land, their first care was to implore God to be propitious, and their last words at parting were solemn prayer and benediction. If he administered medicines for the cure of any disease, he accomplished them with prayer to the God who heals. If he administered even counsel or advice, he would accompany it with prayer to him who disposes the heart to listen, and sometimes he would accompany that prayer with fasting. His best advices, for instance, could not remove some unhappy difference between Lunge and his wife in Rachlin. He therefore adds, "You two and I must spend this day in prayer and fasting." This produced the desired effect, for the penitent wife at length confessed that she found he could obtain from God what to man seemed almost impossible.

In seasons of danger and alarm, whether public or private, he always had recourse to prayer as the most effectual way to prevent, cure, or bear every evil to which man is subject. To better recommend the same course to others, he used to observe and insist upon the return of prayer. Thus, he ascribes it to uncommon wrestling in prayer, that a raging pestilence passed by his monastery. To the same cause (their having prayed and fasted) he ascribes its having carried off only one in the monastery, Baithen. In the 6th century about a third of the human species is computed to have been cut off by pestilence. In the 7th century, also, it raged very much in Britain.

He recommended prayer still further, by representing it as extending its efficacy to future times, and to generations yet unborn. Adomnan gratefully acknowledges that at least Columba's own prayers were in his days productive of signal blessings. "In our time," says he, "we are preserved from another pestilence, so that though it raged through all Europe, it hath not visited our territory; and though we walked, for two years, in the midst of its repeated devastations and ruined villages in England, the kingdom of our good friend Alfred, none of us was ever hurt by it. Thanks be to God, the efficacy of our venerable Father's prayers hath surely reached us." As a side note, the people of Northumberland were converted to the Christian faith in the reign of Oswald, by Aidan and other pious monks of Iona, in consequence of which there was much intercourse between them for a long time after, and many of the churches and monasteries throughout England were planted with divines from this seminary. We learn from Bede that Adomnan, on the occasion here alluded to, had been mediating for a peace between Alfred and his countrymen. He had presented Alfred with a copy of his Description of the Holy Land, and obtained from him many presents. The conversion of Oswald's people is said to have been facilitated by a vision recorded by Adomnan. Before a battle in which Oswald was to engage with Cathon, King of the Britons, he dreamed that he had seen a person of angelic form whose head seemed to reach the clouds, and whose lucid robe covered almost his whole army. This person told him he was Columba and assured him of the victory, which he accordingly obtained. This relation Adomnan had from his predecessor, who had heard it from the mouth of Oswald, who might naturally enough have such a dream upon such an occasion. It may also be said from better authority than Homer that "dreams at times descend from God".

Can anyone conceive such virtue to be in prayer, and not be devoted to it? It is certain none could be more so than Columba, yet he never neglected the use of ordinary means in conjunction with prayer. Thus, at a time when he was in imminent danger at sea, we find him laboring hard in oozing the boat with a bucket, and in the ordinary exercise of his office we have seen that he was far from thinking that the most intense prayer could supersede the necessity of equal intenseness of study. The mariners, however, more pious than many of their brethren in our times, insisted on his betaking himself to his proper business, prayer.

Of the efficacy of intercessory prayer he had the highest opinion, and never failed to recommend and practice it. Accordingly, when he had imitation given him that any person, however distant or unconnected, was in danger of any kind, he would immediately retire to the closet or church to plead in his behalf, or prayed where he was, if the emergency was too sudden to admit of his going elsewhere. The efficacy of prayer depends not on the place, but on the heart, yet the heart we are apt to be impressed more in one place than another. The very sight of a place appropriated to prayer helps to put the pious heart in a praying frame. He would, also, when their case presented itself to his mind, though engaged in company or conversation, dart up sudden and sometimes audible ejaculations in their favor while his change of countenance discovered how much his heart was concerned. The danger of a monk in Durrough had presented itself to his mind.

Nor did he show his sense of the virtue of intercessory prayer only by his own intercessions for others, but also by requesting theirs for him, and by ascribing some of his deliverances more to their prayers than to his own. For instance, being once overtaken by a tempest in the dangerous Gulf of Corryvreckan, and in great danger of being lost, he told those who were with him that he relied more on the intercessions of his friend St. Kenneth, for obtaining a deliverance on that occasion, than on his own prayers. Kenneth knew that his friend was then at sea (as he probably let him know of it, in order to have the benefit of his intercession) and observing the tempest coming on just as he was sitting down to his meat, cried, "It is not the time to eat when Columba is in danger" and flew to the church in such haste that though he had but one of his slippers on, he would not wait to put his foot in the other. This was about the ninth hour; and very soon after the tempest abated, which made Columba afterwards say that they were obliged to Kenneth for not waiting for his shoes. Kenneth died while Abbot of Achabo in Ireland, AD 600. One of the Hebrides near Iona, where he probably resided for some time, still bears his name, and has been lately celebrated in a beautiful Latin ode by Dr. Samuel Johnson, Insula Sancti Kennethi, found in Boswells' book, Journal of a Tour to the Hebrides written in 1785.

Medieval grave slabs produced by the Iona School of West Highland Sculpture, dated fourteenth through early sixteenth century, located on Inch Kenneth.

In order to excite men this to pray for themselves, and intercede for others, he used to observe that God's end in bringing his saints sometimes into danger was to give an opportunity, and to excite themselves and others, to perform this duty with more frequency and greater intenseness. "Though Columan the son of Beogua be just

The stony and seaweed-slicked beach of Inch Kenneth

The chapel ruins of Inch Kenneth

now in such jeopardy in the eddying Gulf of Corryvreckan, lifting both his hands to heaven for assistance, yet God will not leave him to perish, His purpose being only to excite him to pray more fervently for his deliverance."

Thus, in the most unpromising situations, he encouraged a trust in Providence, and cheered men with the hopes of deliverance from their dangers if they prayed and did not faint. This trust he had in

Medieval grave slabs produced by the Iona School of West Highland Sculpture, dated fourteenth through early sixteenth century, located on Inch Kenneth

the highest degree himself, and expressed the highest satisfaction whenever he perceived it firmly fixed in the heart of a disciple.

"A huge sea monster has been seen last night in the course which you are to take today, my dear Baithen, and it may probably meet you."

"And if it should," replied Baithen, "both it and I are in the hands of God."

"Go in peace my son, thy faith is sufficient to save thee from the danger."

Baithen, the cousin, favorite disciple, and immediate successor of Columba as Abbot of Iona, was also much renowned for his wisdom, learning, and sanctity. In a very ancient account of his life it is said that no man ever saw him idle, but always engaged in reading, praying, or working. That next to Columba, he was deemed to be best acquainted with the Scriptures, and to have the greatest extent of learning of any on this side of the Alps. For his zeal, prudence, sanctity, strict discipline, and primitive simplicity of manners, Columba himself used to compare him to John the Evangelist. He was so much given to prayer that even in the necessary intercourse and conversation with his friends, his hands, though concealed under his mantle, might be observed to be every moment lifted up to that praying attitude to which they were so much habituated. Whatever work he was engaged in, his communion with God was so close, and his attention to prayer so constant, that he would not allow so much time as intervened between his swallowing two morsels of meat, or between his reaping a handful of corn and putting it in the sheaf, to pass without his putting up an intercession to Heaven. His humility was such that none could be more careful to conceal his earthly treasures than he was to avoid all ostentation of his heavenly graces. After this account of him, we need not wonder at his biographer hinting that even the devil was obliged to keep his distance and to leave the district of Baithen. On one occasion, however, we find him peeping through the windows, to observe whether each and all in the family devoutly implored the blessing of God upon their meal before they began it, and solemnly returned thanks when they had done. If he still follows this practice (and there is no reason to think that he has slackened his diligence) he must be highly gratified by feeling these matters managed now pretty much in the way that he would wish.

The intercession and prayers of the church, or congregation of Christians, he especially recommended, and regarded so much that on the greatest emergency by night or by day he had always immediate recourse to it. Thus when on a certain day he had notice of Aidan, King of the Scots, one of his friends being about to engage in battle, he quickly ordered the bell to be rung to summon all his monks to the church in order to join their united prayers for victory and safety to King Aidan. Columba judged that when the state protects the church it owes to it in return its prayers and a ready cooperation in maintaining the good order of society. St. Paul directed Christians to pray for kings and rulers, when the king was Nero, and the rulers his cruel instruments of perfection. How much more should the church obey the apostolic precept, when its kings and queens are its nursing fathers and nursing mothers?

Nay, to better recommend the prayers of the church, he ascribed to them not only more efficacy than to those of any one saint, however dear to God, but the power of almost changing the determined purpose of God Himself. One day, as two of his disciples talked to him, they observed his face brightened with unusual and incomparable joy, and in a moment after saw this placid and angelic sweetness of countenance changed into grief and sadness. With difficulty they extorted from him the following account of these various appearances, on condition that they should keep it a secret till after his death:

"Thirty years which I prayed God to give me in Britain, are now expired; and I have much longed and prayed and hoped that at the close of them I should obtain my dismissal and be called to my everlasting home with God, and just now I was above measure glad on feeling the descent of the holy angels to conduct my spirit. But all of a sudden they are stopped at yonder rock, for the united prayers of the churches to spare my life a few years longer have prevailed over my most earnest requests, and changed the purpose of God with regard to me. Four years more I must remain on earth, and then without sickness or pain, this frame shall be dissolved and I shall enter into the joy of my Lord."

It was the custom of Columba, to remark how and when God answered his prayers, and failed not on such occasions to acknowledge His goodness with praise and thanksgiving. Sometimes, too, he would call his friends to join him, especially if they had joined in the request. "My brethren, God hath heard the voice of our supplication at such a time. He hath delivered our friends from danger and it becomes us now to render to Him our united thanks."

But what throws the most beautiful luster on this part of our saint's character, and shows how much his pure spirit was engaged in the high concerns of his ministry, is that even in his sleep his mind, all awake, used to go on with the continuation of those prayers and intercessions which he had been urging at the throne of mercy through the day. When the weakness of the body required rest, the willing spirit still carried on the delightful work and pleaded the cause of his people with his God.

The prayers of Columba were not more remarkable for their frequency than for their fervency, which was strongly marked by his attitude, voice, and countenance. His attitude, though he sometimes stood and was often prostrate, was commonly that of kneeling, with his eyes raised up, and his hands spread towards heaven. From his extreme sensibility of heart and earnestness of spirit, his voice was often attended with cries and tears, and devotion shone in his face with so vivid a luster that the bystanders used to ascribe the uncommon fervency and animation which appeared in it to some irradiation of the Divine Presence upon his countenance, as well as upon his spirit. Who can wonder if a business called The Pleasure of the Lord prospered so astonishingly in the hands of a man so zealous and active, and at the same time so devoted to prayer, and to such prayer too as we have been describing? To the minister who thus liveth, and thus prayeth, all things are possible.

So pious and devout a man as Columba must have been possessed of a heavenly mindfulness rarely to be met with. Accustomed so much to be in company with God, and impressed with so lively a sense of the presence of angels or ministering spirits, he must have been deeply tinctured with their likeness, and in his temper and conduct resembled, while he was yet on earth, the holy inhabitants of heaven. Elevated as he was above every selfish and sublunary view, he had no end or aim but to glorify God and to save souls. It is not therefore without reason that his biographers compare him to one of the prophets or apostles of God, for he had no ordinary share of their spirit.

Besides, it has been already observed that Columba was descended of noble parents, and nearly allied to the royal families of both Scotland and Ireland. He must have had large worldly prospects, if worldly prospects could have allured him. Nay, he seems-from his answer to Sigebert-to have been born not only to large prospects, but to large possessions. Yet of these, as of encumbrances retarding him in his heavenly progress, he divested himself, by allowing them-as we are told by Odonellus-to devolve upon his three uncles, leaving it to their own generosity to give him back such portions as they chose, in order to endow his first monasteries. Hence, when upon some occasion St. Ciaran was considering whether his own zeal for God was equal to that of Columba, for between holy men this was the only rivalship. He was humbled by a dream or vision, in which an angel seemed to have shown him an ax, an emblem of the profession of his father who was a carpenter, saying, "This is what you have given up for the love of God, but Columba has given up a kingdom which was to have come to him by his father."

The uncommon talents, education, and address of Columba, would also qualify him for rising very high in the scale of worldly preferment, if this could attract him. Instead of that, when actually offered him, it could not divert him from the purpose which he had already formed. It would appear that he considered the things of this world, both small and great, as equally beneath his notice except in so far as they contributed to make him more useful and holy and to forward his progress to heaven. Such was the estimate which he seems to have made of this world himself, and which he labored also to impress upon others, teaching the sons of power and ambition that even a kingdom-if obtained at the expense of innocence-was dearly bought and could not be long preserved. He was always exhorting those in humbler stations to never be greatly concerned about the frail and perishing things of the present life.

"Beware, I beseech you, my son," said he to a young ambitious prince, "that you do not attempt to enlarge your possessions by the commission of bloodshed and murder. For if you do, God will soon deprive you and your family of the inheritance of your fathers."

At another time, seeing one of his monks in great grief about a small loss which he had sustained, "Why, my brother," said he, "should you be grieved on account of the loss of such perishing things as these?" And indeed, in this case, the things lost were not the monk's, but Columba's own, so that his exhortation or precept was enforced by his own example.

Thus, in the eyes of Columba, heavenly and divine things shone always with such luster as to darken the brightest objects of human ambition. Objects which he considered and represented as often hurtful rather than useful, to those who attain the largest share of them. Hearing his servant Dermit and another, who traveled with him one day through the dreary wilds of Ardnamurchan, speaking (probably with some envy) of the state of kings, and talking particularly of Beothan and Eachan, two joint kings of Ireland. "O my children," said he, "how empty and unsatisfying are the things you speak of, nay, how pernicious often are they to their owners. For the first account you may probably hear of these kings, is, that their enemies have killed them for the sake of their possessions." On another day, as they were traveling towards Temora, he addressed those who were with him in the same manner. "There is Temora, crowded with people, strong in military power, abounding in nobles, and adorned with a royal palace, and filled with riches and stores of provision! The time is approaching when it shall be left desolate, a monument of the instability of human grandeur. Why should we love or admire the things that are transient and vanishing?"

Indeed all his conversation generally aimed at turning the thoughts of men from earthly things, however great or desirable, to things more durable and solid. Almost every particle of it which is left upon record, and that is not a little, favors heaven and a heavenly turn of mind. His constant tendency is to edify and profit as the cause required, and as opportunity was given. His condescension, affability, and aptness to teach were such that he seemed never at a loss to make every time, place, and person suit his purpose. To every person Columba had something to say, by which he insinuated himself into his favor, and took occasion to edify him, in such a manner as suited his exigency and capacity. If he met but a child, he would ask whose he was and give his benediction. If in the course of his peregrinations he had occasion to meet a poor man, or perhaps to lodge with him in his hut, he would begin perhaps with asking how many cows he had. He would then wish God to bless them until they should become a large fold, and so lead him by degrees to subjects of higher importance. If he should be in the company of nobles or kings, he would give the discourse a tendency either to make themselves good, as we have observed above, or to incline them to do good to others. No other use do we ever find Columba making of his great influence. Meeting one day with a prince of the Orkneys, at the palace of King Brude, he told the king that some monks had lately failed with a view of making discoveries in the northern seas. He begged he would strongly recommend them to the prince who was then with him, in case they should happen to land in the Orkneys. They did so, and owed their lives to the recommendation of Columba. Thus he would never neglect an opportunity of turning the conversation to some purpose that was useful, and of doing good to both the souls and bodies of men. The conversation that was idle he discouraged strongly, though he did it gently, and also the mirth that was unseasonable and unbecoming.

Expeditions of the monks of Iona are frequently mentioned by Adomnan. It is postulated they were in quest of the Thule of the ancients, and observes that the Norwegians found Irish monks in Iceland when they first discovered it about the year 900. Their object undoubtedly was to discover any land which the gospel had not yet reached, that they might preach to its inhabitants the glad tidings of salvation. Nor were they less zealous in rousing men to a greater regard for the truths of the gospel by preaching it in its native purity and simplicity, where it was already professed. We meet with some of them in almost every country in Europe, and their learning and sanctity always procures them respect and honor. The number of them that went to France, Italy, and other foreign countries was so great that the Bollandine writers observe that all saints whose origin could not afterwards be traced were supposed to have come from Ireland or Scotland. The zeal of the monks of Iona disseminating knowledge and true religion, in those dark ages, is indeed astonishing. It flamed in the bosom of aged no less than in the veins of youth.

Cumian, at the age of 70, set out for Italy where he became a bishop, and Columan afterwards bishop of Lindisfarne, could not have set out for England from Iona before he had arrived at the age of 80 as may be inferred from the account of his life by Colgan. The account which Bede gives of Columan and the other divines that went from Hi to England is interesting and curious. They instructed a certain number of the youth, they lived in the most plain and frugal manner, supporting themselves by the labor of their hands, and solicitous only to improve the heart. Except some cattle they had no wealth. If they got any money from the rich they immediately gave it to the poor. Their houses were barely sufficient for their own accommodation, for they never pretended to lodge or entertain the rich, who had nothing to get from them when they came but the Word of God preached in the church. If the king, with five or six attendants, chose at any time to take a refreshment with them after the service was over, he must have contented himself with the plain and daily fare of the brethren. Bede adds that they brought religion at that time into such repute that a clergyman or monk was everywhere received with joy as a servant of God. When they traveled the road people ran to them to get their blessing, and when they went to any village-which they did only when they had occasion to preach, baptize, or visit the sick- crowds gathered to hear them. In short, says he, the cure of souls was their greatest concern.

From the notion which some entertained of Columba being able to foretell future events, a man asked him one day how long he had to live. If your curiosity on that head could be satisfied, said the saint, it could be of no use to you. But it is only God who appoints the days of man; that knows when they are to terminate. Our business is to do our duty, not to pry into our destiny. God in mercy hath concealed from man the knowledge of his end. If he knew it was near, he would be disqualified for the duties of life; and if he knew it were distant, he would delay his preparation. You should therefore be satisfied with knowing that it is certain. The safest way is to believe that it may also be near, and to make no delay in getting ready, lest it overtake you unprepared. Of another, who held a similar conversation with him, he asked how long he thought himself he had to live. The other replied, seven years. Consider then, said he, how much good may be done in such a space of time; but as you know not if it may be seven days, or even seven hours, it is now time to begin and make ready.

So grave and serious was the constant tenor of his conversation that it is said he was never observed to have uttered an idle word, nor to have made the slightest deviation from truth, even in joke or compliment. Odonellus relates that his disciple Baithen declared so to King Aidan, and mentions one or two unsuccessful experiments which were made by the king, to try whether the saint could be made to deviate from the strict account given of him. Columba commanded the respect of kings by speaking the truth, and the truth only, without using any idle words, compliment, or flattery. Aodh, King of Ireland, asked him whether he thought he should be saved. You have little chance for that, said Columba, unless you expiate the errors of your past life by a speedy and sincere repentance and by the exercise of good works for the future.

As the conversation of Columba was heavenly, so his life and actions were alike useful and holy. Everything he did was suitable to his profession, and bespoke the man of God. When we consider his devotion we should almost think he had left no room for activity; and when we consider his usefulness and activity, we shall almost think that he had no time left for devotion. But they both harmonized so sweetly, that instead of interfering they mutually served to assist each other. And indeed the only way to do much business is to be much in prayer, especially in the sacred office. In any office, to be good and to do good are but one and the same study, though too many think they may be separately pursued. In Columba they were both so intimately united that holiness unto the Lord and usefulness to man were stamped on all his actions.

How much his character was marked with the first of these we have already seen, and the other is equally manifest, from his having been constantly engaged in doing all the good in his power to the souls and bodies of men. From pure love to the souls of men he gave up every worldly prospect and profession, and submitted to a life of the utmost self-denial, toil, danger, and anxiety. With what activity and zeal he labored for the souls of men we need no other evidence than the great and rapid success of his ministry. For close application and activity he was indeed noted from his early youth. When he studied under Finnian, every night on which it fell to his share to grind the corn with the quern or hand mill, he did it so expeditiously that his companions alleged that he had always the assistance of an angel in turning the stone and envied him much on that account. His future life is marked with the same close application and diligence. He slept little, was never idle, and never employed about anything that was useless. In a life so busy and by a soul animated with zeal for the glory of God and the salvation of souls, he hath shown how much may be accomplished. His zeal, like that of the ministers above, was indeed a flame of fire: strong, active, penetrating, and cheering. It not only moved him to devote his life to God, but to fill every moment of that life with labor and action. Insomuch that with watching and praying and the discharge of the other various parts of his ministry, he lived to all purposes of such a life, more in one day that ordinary pastors perhaps in many weeks or months. It is not by sitting still and going through set exercises at stated times that ministers can hope to make conversions. Columba did not so make his. Unweariedly and incessantly we find him going about, through his immense charge or diocese, from house to house, and from kingdom to kingdom. Wherever he is, every word, every deed, proclaims the minister diffusing everywhere the blessings of the gospel, establishing grace in souls, and peace in families.

It has been already observed that the saint had always something suitable to say the every person of every age and condition. Yet he seems to have paid the most particular attention to the young, well aware of the importance of early piety, and of the greater probability of succeeding in his endeavors to impress a sense of religion when he had to work on tender souls. The young, therefore, he regarded with particular care. He encouraged them to come to him on all occasions and to share in his instruction, prayers, and benedictions. Even before they were capable of learning, he wished to cultivate their acquaintance and to conciliate their favor by the most endearing tenderness. By having their affections pre-engaged, he might afterwards the more easily convey his instructions. Hence, when the saint makes his appearance, the little children rejoice to see him, and they run to meet him, and he embraces them and takes them in his bosom. If only the elder children of the family should be presented to him, he would say, "Have you not some that are younger than these? I wish to see them." They are all sent for, and little Eachan Bui, when he saw the saint, ran up to him and laid his head on his bosom. The saint affectionately kissed him, blessed him, hoped he would survive his father, and afterwards leave children to succeed him. How amiable is the saint when thus courting the affections of children! How lovely is old age and holiness this delighting to associate themselves to infancy!

As the happiness of multitudes depends on the temper and character of those who are destined to fill the higher ranks of life, he attended more especially to such, had them often with him, endeavored to impress their minds with a just opinion of worldly greatness, and to inspire them with the love of peace, the force of long life to themselves, and of happiness to those about them. By this I mean not that Columba had any respect of persons in any of his sacred ministrations. In what related only to the individual, and did not affect the interests of society at large, the souls and persons of the lowest shared in his labors and concern, as well as those of the highest. The family mentioned above, in which he spent a day of fasting and prayer with a view to establish peace in it, and about which he was so anxiously concerned that his soul went on with the intercession of the day during the sleep of the night, is mentioned to have been of the lower rank or plebeian order.

Columba indeed, like a true minister of the Prince of Peace, and of that Gospel which proclaims it, labored for nothing so much as to bring this blessing not only to families and to individuals but even to kingdoms. In the great council of Drimceat, already mentioned, he mediated so effectually between the Scottish and Irish kings, that both agreed to refer their respective claims to his own decision. This he modestly, and perhaps wisely declined, that he might not incur the displeasure of either but persuaded them to refer the matter to Colman the son of Comgel, a man well versed in sacred and profane literature, and especially in the antiquities of Ireland. His great influence was in like manner exerted in preserving peace between the Scots and Picts and in composing their differences, when any difference arose. Equally respected by both, we find him going backwards and forwards from the one court to the other, always zealous and always successful in his endeavors to prevent or terminate the dire calamities of war. Thus, by his great influence, he often saved a torrent of bloodshed both in Scotland and Ireland. The fame deference was paid to his counsels in both kingdoms, and the most momentous affairs often referred to his decision. Cairbre, the son of Lugid Lamdarg, missing a stroke aimed at a stag, killed his brother-which gave rise to a violent contest between him and a remaining brother about the inheritance of the one that was killed. In vain did the king and clergy of Ireland attempt to settle the difference. The contending parties, however, agreed to refer it to the decision of Columba. They accordingly came, with a numerous train to Iona, where the saint reconciled them and saved Ireland from a civil war. Happy would it be for every age if the quarrels of kings and kingdoms could be settled, as they were then, by being referred to such an umpire.

There was nothing about which Columba was more anxious, or in which he was more successful, than in maintaining peace in all the churches and religious societies under his care. Nor was there anything that seemed to give him so much concern as the apprehensions which he had that his peace might one day be disturbed, by such foolish disputes as those which afterwards took place concerning the feast of Easter. Columba however maintained the peace of the church in his day, and with his dying breath left it in charge to his disciples to have peace among themselves.

How ardently he loved peace may be inferred from its having been one of the three things which, on a particular occasion, he is said to have solemnly asked of God at Tulach nan Salm (the Hill of Psalms). The first was that he might never refuse any person in a reasonable demand lest this should hurt his usefulness, the second that the love and zeal which he had for God in his heart should never be abated, and the third that all his friends and relations might live in amity and peace among themselves and if at any time they should not, that God would rather punish the fault himself than allow them to hurt one another.

But this love of peace in Columba never hindered him from exercising the strictest discipline and order, well knowing that without this no lasting peace could be maintained. He admonished and reproved with freedom and when the case required it, with sharpness. If that did not serve, without any regard to persons, he proceeded to higher censures. Thus, at the hazard of his life, he excommunicated some of the nobility of the kingdom (the sons of Connel) after having first admonished and reproved them to no purpose. Nay, when he saw no prospect of their reformation, after every mean of reclaiming them was tried, he seems to have thought it mercy to their own souls as well as society to request of God, if He had no purpose of mercy in reserve for them, to shorten the time of their doing mischief and to check by His Providence the evil which could not be restrained by either law or religion.

These cases, however, were very rare and extremely desperate, in which we find the saint proceeding to this last appeal. John, one of the excommunicated sons of Connel, continued to persecute and harass the good, and to live by rapine and plunder. Thrice had he robbed the house, and carried off the effects of a worthy hospitable man who used to lodge the saint whenever he came his way. On the third time Columba met him as he was carrying off his booty, and earnestly entreated him to leave it. He followed him all the way to his boat (which lay at Camus in Ardnamurchan) and even waded after him into the sea with his fruitless petitions. The plunderer and his company (which seem to have been of much the same cast with his followers on a former occasion, when one of them attempted to kill Columba) scorned and laughed at him. The saint at length, lifting both his hands to heaven, prayed to God to glorify Himself by avenging and protecting His people. He then sat down on an eminence and thus addressed a few who were along with him, "God will not always bear to have those who love and serve Him to be thus treated. That dark cloud already forming in the north is fraught with his poor man's destruction." The cloud spread, the storm arose between Mull and Colonfay, and it overtook and sunk the boat which no doubt the greed of plunder had too deeply loaded. His fate, though just, is much to be lamented.

If Columba was attentive to keep discipline and order among his people, much more was he solicitous to do so among his clergy. He seems indeed to have had nothing more at heart than to promote the purity and usefulness of the sacred order, and therefore he paid always the strictest regard to whatever related to their ordination and discipline. He appears to have been not only careful to examine into their talents, views, morals, and earlier habits of life, but even anxious to know if they were born of pious parents. He might probably reckon on something of the nature of the flock being communicated to the scion, as well as on the effect of good example, early discipline, and timeous instructions in piety. On this last account he was particularly anxious to know if the mother, who has the first molding of the soul in the cradle, was herself truly religious and holy. Whenever he discovered any young person of parts and piety he was particularly careful to cherish them himself, to recommend them to others, and in due time to promote them, when their parts were well cultivated and their piety well proved. He himself was from his earliest years inflamed with ardent zeal to attain to Christian perfection, and he reckoned piety in youth to be the best, if not the only, security for sanctity and usefulness in riper years.

Of how much importance he thought it to have churches supplied with such pastors as has been distinguished for their early piety, appears from the earnestness with which a short time before his death he recommended to his successor the care and promotion of a young man of whom he had justly, on this account, conceived the highest hopes. "Take particular heed, I beseech you, Baithen, to what I am now to say to you. After I shall be with Christ, which I earnestly look and long for, a youth of parts, piety, and study, named Finten, will readily come over from Ireland and make one of your monks. But I beg you may not detain him here. Let him be the father of a monastery in Leinster, where he will faithfully feed the flock of Christ and lead very many souls to glory."

When any other probationer had not turned his attention to the ministry till he was far advanced in life, and consequently wanted those advantages which early habits of study and early devotedness to the sacred office might furnish, or when the character or qualifications of such were anyhow doubtful, he was remarkably cautious of receiving them, till they were long tried and gave satisfying evidences of their fitness. A man of this description came to him one day from Connaught, requesting to be put in orders. The saint, after some questioning and examination, seemed rather desirous to divert him from his purpose, however well he might have thought of his intentions. With this view he set before him the strictness of his monastic rule, and all the hardships and labors to which the sacred life was subject. The candidate heard them all without being in the least staggered. Be it so then, says Columba, but before I administer the vows to you, I require of you first to spend seven years of probation in a monastery to which I shall send you, that of Achaluing in Ethica. The long course of education and probation required of his disciples by Columba must have contributed much to their usefulness, as well as to the fame which they acquired for learning when the clergy of other parts of Europe were woefully ignorant. In the life of St. Munn, one of Columba's disciples, it is mentioned that his education took up eighteen years, in which there is no reason to think that he was singular.

As he was thus careful himself about the piety, parts, preparation, and views of those whom he admitted to the sacred office, so was he much grieved and moved with uncommon indignation when he heard of any unworthy person having been ordained or admitted to the ministry by another. Being one day informed that Aodh du' mac Sui'ne, a man of high descent but a regicide long inured to crimes, had professed to change his mode of life and had been afterwards admitted into holy orders, he uttered the following dreadful sentence-which Adomnan delivers as a prophecy-and says it was all fulfilled. "Perish the hand which Finchan laid upon that cursed head, and let it be dead and buried while himself is yet alive. As for Aodh, he will return to his former course of life as a dog to vomit, and be killed as he did kill by the edge of the sword."

To preserve the purity of his monks, and indeed of all good men, he taught them as a matter of the highest consequence, to avoid as much as possible the company and conversation of the wicked, when their character was such as did not afford any prospect of their being reclaimed. His own practice was to have as little intercourse as possible with such, no further than necessity or piety required. Observing one day a man of this hopeless stamp about to land on his island, he immediately sent Dermit with orders not to allow him to set foot on the isle but to send him instantly back to Mull. On the other hand, he so strongly recommended the company of the good and urged so much the advantage of having them always for associates, that he ascribed Cormac's want of successes in an undertaking of great importance to his not taking with him a man of much piety who wished to attend him. The zeal of Columba's disciples to discover unknown countries in which they might propagate the gospel was noticed before, and for this zeal no one was more distinguished than Cormac, whose voyages into the ocean are often mentioned by Adomnan. Indeed all of them seemed to have the same spirit. One of them, St. Mochon, being urged by his father to remain in his native country, replied, "You are indeed my father, but the Church is my mother. Wherever I can reap the best harvest, and do most service to the cause of Christ, that I consider as my country."

After what has been said, it is almost unnecessary to add that no one ever showed greater affection and regard to such of the sacred order as lived and acted according to the spirit of their office. To them he seldom or never speaks without using the most tender and endearing names of brother, son, or child, or blessed, or some other expression of the same amount. But when he heard of any of them being openly profane, or formal and hypocritical in their profession, or inattentive to the authority, dignity, and gravity becoming their sacred character, or countenancing and giving their preference to vain and idle amusements, though they should not otherwise share in them, he failed not to denounce against them above all sinners the heaviest judgements of heaven. Such was his sense of the sanctity of the office, his love for the souls of men, and his zeal for the service of God, that he could never see an unworthy person in this office without expressing the strongest indignation. Seeing once an unholy priest officiate in celebrating the Eucharist, though he was not in his jurisdiction, he could not help being moved so far as to cry out, "Ah! What a combination of clean and unclean things is here! The symbols of Christ administered by wicked hands."

It would be doing great injustice to the character of Columba not to observe, that through his zeal, at some rare times, was thus moved with indignation against enormous vice, or clerical profanities, yet he was habitually a man of great meekness and sweetness of temper who had brought all his passions to subjection, and ruled his tongue by the strictest reins. This, if we had no other evidence for it, might easily be inferred from the general esteem and regard of all ranks for him, especially of his monks and servants. This general love and regard is seldom procured by the severer virtues, or even by good offices alone, they must be accompanied by the softer graces of affability, meekness, condescension, and tenderness. For, though we may give our love only to the latter, and these Columba possessed in a very high degree. All persons, rich or poor, who had occasion to see him, or even to solicit him in regard to the concern of soul or body, were sure of being received with a tender and cordial embrace. Of being treated during their converse with every possible mark of benevolence, and dismissed with the most affectionate farewell and benediction. Every caution which a deep concern for their welfare could suggest, he would give before he could part with them. "This day, I beseech you my son, take not the straight course to Ethica, but rather sail round by the coast and small islands, for there are some whales in the channel and I cannot think of your being in fear or danger." This Ethica, often mentioned by Adomnan, is most likely the island of Eig which lays to the north of Iona.

Indeed, the near interest which Columba took in everything that concerned his friends was so great that he himself considered it as a frailty. This amiable virtue, he thought, might carry off his attention too much from the contemplation and pursuit of divine and heavenly objects. For even when out of his sight, his friends and acquaintance were always present to his mind, insomuch that if the wind but changed, he considered how that change might affect them and consequently how he should pray or praise in regard to them. "Fourteen days now has the wind been from the north since Cormac left us. The danger to which he is driven, far beyond the reach of land, must surely be extreme. Let us, my brethren, go all to the church and earnestly intercede with God on his behalf." There, with bended knee and weeping voice, he prays to Him who rules the wind, and when it changes, he gratefully returns to render thanks.

Towards his monks he always behaved with such meekness and love, as endeared his person to them so much, that any of them would willingly save his life at the expense of his own and perform whatever he desired, though at the hazard of perishing in the attempt. When he addressed them, it was always with the compellation of "brethren" or "children." When any of them offended himself, he forgave him, when any of them offended God, he prayed for him. His affection for them indeed was so great that he could hardly deny them any request, even the most unreasonable. When two of his monks, on a certain occasion, wished to know the cause of that wonderful joy which they perceived in his countenance, he strongly but softly checked their curiosity and expressed his extreme unwillingness to disclose what he wished to keep secret. "Depart in peace, I beseech you, and do not urge me further about this affair." They clung to his knees, they wept, they humbly entreated him to comply. "I cannot see you so sad, because I love you," said he, "and will tell you, in the confidence that you will not, at least in my lifetime, reveal it." Is not this the picture of a meek and tender parent, with his little children around him?

Even his domestics, or working monks and servants, he generally addressed by the tender compellation of "little children" and instead of reproving them for any fault which did not proceed from design, would rather excuse and comfort them. One of them being ordered one day for Ireland, allowed the tide to carry away the leathern bottle (which he had for holding his milk) while it was steeping within the sea mark. His master saw his concern, and said to him, "My brother, be not concerned, tomorrow when the tide returns, we may probably find the bottle."

Towards Dermit especially, his pious and constant attendant, he discovers on all occasions the affection of a parent than the authority of a master. With what tender concern, for instance, does he hang over his bed when he was thought at the point of death, and how earnestly does he request of God to heal and spare his servant Dermit, as long as he himself should remain in the present world? His prayer was heard, and for at least thirty four years, to the honor of both, he and Dermit lived together and we may believe that death could not long divide them. Every part of Columba's domestic character is marked with sensibility and tenderness. Even in the necessary labors imposed upon his monks, his feeling soul took a share and ministered to them every consolation in his power. For this purpose would he visit them at their work, carried in a wain or wheel carriage, when by reason of age or infirmity he could not go otherwise, so that their joy and happiness in his service was by themselves confessed to be greater than they could express by language. From the toil of the day they always returned home cheerful and glad at night, and from the love which they bore to their master they felt not the weight of their burden. There is something, said one of the oldest of them, which makes me so happy and glad, that even when I am bearing this burden I do not perceive the weight of it.

For the monks of other monasteries, even in the most distant of his jurisdiction, he had the same tender regard. He entered deeply into their joy or sorrow, grieving when they were grieved, and rejoicing when they rejoiced. On a certain winter's day, which was exceedingly cold, the saint was observed to be in the utmost distress, and even to weep bitterly. His servant, Dermit, took the liberty to ask the cause of his sorrow and got the following answer, "It is not without reason, my child, that I am this day so sad. My monks in Durrough are, at this inclement season, sadly oppressed by Laisran, who keeps them at hard labor to build him a larger house." Soon after he learned that Laisran had relented, and put a stop to the work till the weather should be milder, upon which he rejoiced exceedingly, communicated the glad tidings to his brethren, and blessed the relenting heart of Laisran.

The tenderness and sensibility of Columba were indeed exquisite, and easily interested him not only in what concerned his friends and domestics, but any part of the human race however distant. One evening, as one of the monks came to speak to him after grinding the corn, he observed his master's countenance (which always used to be serene, cheerful, and pleasant) so full of terror and concern, that he ran hastily back, greatly alarmed, and unable to account for extraordinary and unusual an appearance. After a little time, however, he took courage, went back, and requested to know the cause. The saint told him that he had just learned that a city of Italy was destroyed by lightning, by which above three thousand souls had perished.

To those who were nearer hand, Columba gave more substantial proofs of his regard than outward signs. He discharged every social duty with the utmost care, doing good to all, and giving cause of offense to no one. His caution in this last respect was extremely great. His monks had one day cut some stakes and wands to repair their houses. Such houses were afterwards plastered with clay and made no uncomfortable habitations. Adomnan mentions that a celestial light was seen to dart through the keyhole of a house in which Columba had been privately praying, from which it may be inferred that the house had no other chinks in it, otherwise this would not have been particularly mentioned. The reason that we see so few remains of buildings prior to the use of lime is because many of them were constructed in this manner. The sides as well as roof of the monk's houses were made of wicker, or wands woven on stakes. The possessor of the ground from which they were taken was somewhat displeased, although such things were at that time, and for ages after, considered as no man's property and indeed of no value in a country overrun with wood. Yet the saint, when he heard of it, could not bear to have any man offended, and therefore immediately sent him a valuable present of barley for feed, and to enhance its value and show his benevolence, he sent his benediction along with it.

In every shape, indeed, his benevolence exerted itself towards all within his reach, and moved him to compassion alike the souls and bodies of men. If they were in prison, he visited and comforted them. If in bondage, he redeemed them. Silver and gold, it is true, he had not often, but what he had he cheerfully gave away. A valuable spear, embellished with ivory, is the price of one, and restoring the sick master to health is done on condition of obtaining release to another, contrary to his usual practice of giving his trouble, skills, and medicine freely. Slavery is utterly inconsistent with the spirit of the gospel, and so hostile to it was Columba, that contrary to his usual practice he not only refused to give medicines to a master that was sick, but also assured him that his disease would soon prove fatal if he did not accept the condition upon which he offered his assistance and give liberty to his female slave, which till then he could not prevail with him to do. Of slaves or captives there seem to have been but a few instances in the jurisdiction of Columba, and his zeal in their behalf must have soon procured their liberty. We do not find that this kind of slavery prevailed afterwards in the Highlands. In Ireland it did, and Giraldus Cambrenfis says that a general convocation of clergy in 1170, the calamities which the Irish had suffered were ascribed to their having been in the practice of buying slaves from England, partly stolen and partly sold by their parents, and that it was then ordained that all the English slaves in Ireland should have their liberty. Colgan, who cites the passage, wishes the English would, in their turn, follow this example, left as they were deeper in the guilt, their punishment would be more severe.

Whenever Columba heard any was in sickness, he not only visited him and prayed for him, and that too with such tender emotion as showed how much his heart was affected, but also administered medicines with which he often sent messengers as far as other kingdoms. When the ailments of his patients were of such a nature as to allow them to travel, he encouraged them to come and stay with him, that he might be the better enabled to understand their diseases. And that, if he could not restore them to health, he might at least prepare them for dying. The value of an immortal soul, capable of everlasting happiness or endless misery, he knew to be inconceivably great, and the right improvement of the few precious moments allowed by heaven for its probation to be a matter of unspeakable consequence. If, therefore, he might help anyone whose moments of grace had not yet expired, to form one good purpose, perform one good deed, or if he could not excite one pious sentiment in their soul, he knew it would be of more value than if he could give them a kingdom. Such opportunities, therefore, as conferred the power of doing this, he eagerly fought for. When the duty of residence (with which he seems unwilling to dispense but when the reason was great and urgent) did not permit his going from his charge at home, he wished to have those who approached near their end brought to where he was. Go, said he to two of his monks, to the cell of Diun, at Loch-ava, and tell Cailtan to make no delay in coming hither. Cailtan came, and the saint told him that as he understood his life was near a close, he wished to have him with himself that as a lover and friend of his soul, he might help him to finish his course with the greater comfort. He died within a week.

Such was the hospitality of Columba that without being sent for, anyone might come and assuredly rely on being made welcome, not only for days but for months or years, if this were to do him service. Two strangers, on a certain Sabbath day, cried on the other side of the little firth that separates Hy from Mull. "Make haste," said Columba, "and bring the strangers over." They came, the saint saluted them, and

Looking from Iona towards Mull

having inquired into the cause of their coming, they told him that they came with an intention to remain with him during that year. The saint probably perceiving that their state of health would not permit them to live so long (as he hinted to some others) recommended to them to enter into their number, and to commence the life of monks. They did so, and died within the space of a month.

Hospitality, in a country thinly inhabited, and in a rude state of society, is a virtue of the first order. Columba therefore recommended it strongly by his preaching, and enforced it by the sanction of promises and threats, but more especially by his own example-without which the preacher must always preach in vain. Besides, Columba's manner of discharging this duty, and his attentions to his guests, were such as to greatly enhance the merit of the performance. Before the guests have yet arrived, he orders the water to be got ready for bathing their feet to refresh them after the fatigues of the journey, and like a true minister of that religion which prefers mercy to sacrifice, he dissolves even the solemnity of a fast, for the sake of discharging the duty of hospitality to the weary and hungry traveler. This fast was said to have been on the fourth day of the week, Wednesday, and called the "customary fast" whence it appears that they kept on this day a weekly fast, a practice which Colgan says continued in the Irish church till the beginning of the fifteenth century. The day observed by the Roman church was Friday. Adomnan calls the days of the week by their cardinal number, after the Lord's Day, not by their Roman names.

Columba's own regard to hospitality and its vast necessity and value in such places and times may account for the high indignation which a man of so meek and mild a spirit expressed upon an occasion on which its sacred laws were most atrociously broken, and the crime complicated with murder. Taran, a Pictish exile of noble descent, was anxiously recommended by the saint for a few months to the care of a powerful man in Italy of the name of Feradach. Instead of protecting as he promised, Feradach ordered him after some few days to be put to the sword. The saint, who probably considered himself as accountable for the exile, soon heard of his having been murdered by Feradach, and thus gave vent to his emotion, "It is not to me, but to God, that the poor unhappy man hath lied. His name shall be blotted out of the book of life. It is now midsummer, and in autumn, before he shall have tasted the flesh of his hogs, after they shall have fed upon the nuts, he shall suddenly die and suffer the just reward of his crimes." Feradach hoped to belie the prophecy the earliest nuts, and killing a boar which ate some of them, before the usual time. But on the very day, or rather at that very instant, when it was just brought to him, and when he thought to have tasted of it, according to Adomnan, he fulfilled the prediction.

This, and or two similar denunciations in the life of Columba, will be ascribed by some to a prophetic impulse, and by others to a spark of passion, struck even out of a sanctified heart, by the collision of a very strong provocation. Accordingly, some will perhaps place them to the score of merit, and others to that of defect or foible. I shall only observe that whatever may be thought of these instances, Columba's ordinary and habitual frame of spirit was of the most forgiving nature. Few, if any, ever gave him more trouble or opposition than the Pictish priest, or Druidh, Broichan. Broichan had the merit of dealing in a more open and avowed manner than some of his brethren. Odonellus relates that when Columba first landed in Iona, on Pentecost eve, some druids who had been there disguised themselves in the habit of monks, and pretended they had come to that place to preach the gospel, with a request that he and his followers might betake themselves to some other place, but that Columba immediately discovered the imposter and then they resigned the field to him. Yet despite this, when Columba heard as he traveled near his place of residence, that this man was thought to be dying, he made all possible expedition to heal him. And though it is well known that the bards in Columba's time were becoming a nuisance to society in general, and extremely adverse to the views of those who propagated the Christian religion. Yet at the great council of Drimeeat, when all the other members unanimously agreed upon their being put to death and an end being put to the order, Columba alone interceded in their behalf, and by his great influence the bards were saved. The bards, from their connection with the druids whose superstition was to be set aside, were very troublesome to the first preachers of Christianity, some of whom were not dispossessed to show them the same charity with Columba. Poor St. Columba was so provoked by them as to wish at length that the earth might swallow them as it did Korah. But Columba was not only fond of their poetry and a poet himself, but of a different spirit, though he too was often teased by them. Odonellus mentions one occasion on which they threatened to lampoon him for not giving them, when at the time he had nothing about him to bestow, and such was his tender regard for his character, that he was obliged to wipe the sweat from his face with his hand, before he got clear of them. Afterwards, however, they were very grateful for his intercession in their favor, and Dallan, the chief of them, exerted all his skill to praise him. When he had recited but a part of the poem to the saint, who seemed to be much pleased with it, Baithan, fearing that even his master might be elated with the praise, as well as pleased with the poetry, put him upon his guard by telling him that he saw a black cloud of evil spirits hovering over his head. Columba took the hint, ordered the poet to stop, and never to repeat the poem afterwards, adding that no man should be praised until he had reached the goal and finished the course. Dallan waited till Columba did so, and then published his poem which was well known in Ireland by the name of Ambra Cholum-chille, or the Eulogy of Columkille.

When the injury or provocation was directly offered to himself, he was equally ready to forgive, and even to return his enemies good for evil. A thief had gone from Colonsay to Mull, with a view of carrying away some of the saint's property on a small adjoining island. Before he could get off, he was discovered, apprehended, and brought to the saint, who thus addressed him, "Why do you thus go on in the practice of stealing your neighbor's goods and breaking the commandment of God? For the future, come to me whenever you are in need, and you shall have what you have occasion for." At the same time he ordered some wedders to be killed and given him; that he might not return empty to his poor family. And learning soon after that he was not likely to live long, he ordered a fat mutton and six measures of corn to be sent to him, which as he died about the time in which the supply arrived, served the occasion of his funeral.

It is only in those cases in which sinners were past all hopes of reformation that Columba gave them up, and even then his severe sentence might be uttered as the last effort of a gracious spirit to rouse and to reclaim them. If, after all, sinners went on and died impenitent (an event which we cannot suppose his threats would hasten) no man could be more grieved. The severest groans that ever broke from his heart were those to which he gave vent when he heard of sinners having died in their impenitence.

But when any person repented of his sins, none could possibly show more regard and tenderness. On the top of the eminence about his monastery Columba sat one day, looking out most anxiously for the appearance of a sail from Ireland. Dermit was near him, and to him he expressed his concern at not seeing a vessel which he expected to arrive on that day, with a man who had fallen into some grievous sin, for which he now labored under the sincerest sorrow and repentance. Dermit soon after told him that he perceived a sail making towards the port. Then, said the saint, let us quickly rise and meet the penitent, for Christ Himself receives the penitent. Fechnus landed, Columba ran to embrace him, mingled his tears of joy with the tears of sorrow shed by the other, while he thus addressed him, "My son, I beseech thee take comfort. The sins which thou hast committed are forgiven, for it is written a broken and a contrite heart God will not despise."

In speaking of the benevolence and tenderness of Columba's heart, we must not omit his charity in relieving and procuring relief for the needy, by every method in his power besides praying for the blessing of God to increase their store. In one of the accounts of his life, published by Colgan, we are told that after he had erected the monastery of Durrough he ordered a hundred poor persons to be served with victuals every day at a certain hour, and appointed an almoner for that purpose. One day a mendicant came to apply for a share of this charity, but was told by the almoner that he could have nothing as the appointed number had been already served. He came the second day, and was told in like manner that he was come too late, and that for the future he must come earlier, if he expected his share of the charity. The third day, however, he came as late as before, and when the almoner gave him the same reply as formerly, he bade him go and tell from him to the abbot that he ought not to limit his charity by any precise rules which God had not prescribed, but always to give while he had, in whatever number, time, or manner, the poor should apply to him. Columba, upon receiving this message, ran hastily after the mendicant, who had then assumed a heavenly form, which gave him to understand to whom he was indebted for the counsel. From that day forward he laid aside his rules and gave to all objects, at all times, provided he had anything to bestow. If at any time he had not, his tears would flow, till God enabled him to relieve their wants. Hence, adds the writer, he was esteemed what he really was, the common father and patron of the poor and needy.

Next the salvation of souls, the object which most engaged the heart of Columba was charity. St. Mobith, who had just built a church, brought St. Ciaran, St. Kenneth, and St. Columba to see it and desired each of them to say with what things he would have it filled if he has his wish. Ciaran, who spoke first, said he would wish to have it filled with holy men ardently engaged in celebrating the praises of God. Kenneth said his wish would be to have it filled with sacred books, which should be read by many teachers who would instruct multitudes, and stir them up to the service of God. And I, said Columba, would wish to have it filled with silver and gold, as a fund for erecting monasteries and churches, and for relieving the necessities of the poor. And to you, said Mobith, God will give the power to do what you now wish to perform.

Even Baithen, who had so much of the spirit of his master, thought that Columba sometimes rather exceeded in the exercise of almsdeeds, or charity. One day as the reapers were employed in cutting the corn, Baithen came home before them to see if their victuals were ready, and was much dissatisfied at finding that Columba had given to the hungry the most of what had been made ready for the reapers. But his master, with a mild and tranquil voice, told him that God would repay with interest whatever was given away for his sake, and that he would find that what remained would, with God's blessing, be enough to satisfy the reapers.

Of all Columba's virtues, indeed, none was more conspicuous than charity. He never saw any man, in any distress, without doing all he could to relieve him. Nothing grieved him more than to see a rich man void of charity to the poor, and evil which he labored so much to cure that, on one occasion, we find him refusing to partake of a rich man's entertainment till he brought him to a sense of his sin and to a promise of amendment. His detestation of avarice is strongly marked by an incident recorded by Odonellus. Two mendicants, the one noted for his careful and the other for his dissipated turn of mind, applied to him at the same time for charity. To the first he gave a little money, but to the last a great deal more. Some who were with him at the time, expressed their disapprobation at his giving most to the one who, in their opinion, was the least deserving. Columba desired them to inquire what use each made of what he gave them. They did so, and found that the first, who happened to die immediately after, had put up what he got with ten pieces of gold which he had sewed in his garment; while the other had taken the first opportunity of spending what he had got and giving all about him a liberal share of what he had purchased.

In any of the sacred order especially, he was so shocked at seeing a want of charity to the poor, or that avaricious and tenacious turn of mind from which it springs, that this made one of the rare provocations which made him lose the calm tenor of his soul and for a moment give place to the feelings of an indignant spirit. "Gallan, one of the clergy of your diocese," said he to Bishop Colgion, "I understand is just now dead. His heart was hard and avaricious, and his soul is now with devils."

On the other hand, he showed the highest regard, and gave the warmest commendation, to every person of distinguished charity. Here, said he on a very public occasion, is the gift of a rich man who has mercy for the poor, and therefore mercy shall eternally reward his bounty. He was particularly delighted when at any time he discovered a high degree of this amiable virtue in a man of mean or ordinary circumstances. In the inland parts of Scotia, says Adomnan, lived Colum Coilrin, a smith by occupation, remarkable for his virtues, and above all, much given to alms-deeds and charity. In an advanced age he died, of which Columba, having got immediate notice, thus spoke to those who were with him at the time, "Happy man! Who, with the labor of his hands, hath obtained from God such eternal rewards in heaven, for, whatever he could make of his trade that he gave to the poor in charity. And now his soul is conducted by the holy angels to the glory and joy of the celestial paradise."

Compassion, indeed, was so strongly marked on the soul of Columba, that he was disposed on all occasions to exercise it, not only to his own species but to every creature under heaven. Some person had once the presumption to request of him to bless his dagger. "God grant, then," said the saint, "that it may never shed a drop of the blood of either man or beast." The following incident will further illustrate this part of Columba's character: a crane had one day taken its flight across the seas from Ireland, and by the time it drew near the shore of Iona, was so spent that it was obliged to alight in the water. The saint foresaw that this was likely to be its fate, and had already ordered one of his monks away, though it was at the most distant part of the island, to take up the poor bird and save its life. Bring it, said he, to the nearest house, feed it, and take all the care you can of it for three days, till it be well refreshed, and recover its strength, so as to be able to cross the sea again to its native home. The monk obeyed, and the saint was thankful. "For this act of mercy and hospitality, may God command on thee His blessing, my dear brother." What a beautiful picture have we in this chapter of the benevolence of Columba.

Another incident of the like nature occurs in the account which we have of the transactions of the saint's dying day. He had been to see and to bless the provision of his monks, from whom he was on that day to be taken away. On his return to the monastery, he sat down on the way to rest. His old white horse, which used to carry the milk vessels betwixt the monastery and the fold, observed him, came where he was, reclined his head upon his breast, and, as if sensible of his master's near departure, began to express his grief by groans and even tears. Dermit offered to turn him away, but the saint forbade. "Let him alone" said he, "let him alone, for he loves me, and I will not hinder him on this occasion to drop his tears in my bosom, and show the bitterness of his grief. To thee God hath given reason, but see (that they might not be despised) He hath planted affection even in brutes, and in this even, something like a prescience of my departure. Now, my faithful and affectionate friend, be gone, and may you be kindly cared for by Him who made you!"

It is with particular pleasure I observe in how high a degree Columba possessed another and higher species of charity than that which I have been speaking of. By this I mean the liberality and candor of his sentiments in allowing a share in the portions of the blessed to the truly virtuous of every persuasion. When men, unenlightened by the gospel, lived according to the light of nature and of conscience (dim as it was), God, he believed, would accept them for their having improved the talent which they received without exacting of them any account of the talent which they received not. The honest Heathen, who had a disposition to receive the gospel, if he had a tender of it, obtains at his disposal like the Christian saint, a convoy of holy angels. Traveling one day along the side of Loch Ness, and having got intelligence of a worthy Heathen in the neighborhood being at the point of death, he made no scruple to say to those about him, that the angels were already come down from heaven to conduct the soul of that man to glory. At the same time he did not think it unnecessary, at least not improper, to hasten his pace and if he could overtake it, give him an opportunity which he probably heard the man had wished for, of being initiated into the Christian faith by baptism.

It deserves to be noticed, as a matter very congenial to this candor of soul, that Columba is said to have forever maintained a cheerfulness of countenance and an angel-like aspect, which strongly attracted the love of the beholder. At the same time it showed how much his soul was filled with that heavenly joy, which is the fruit of the spirit, and the present portion of the genuine sons of God. Some may perhaps think that the austere and mortified life which Columba led was inconsistent with this cheerfulness of aspect and joy of spirit. But if we make a due allowance for the difference of the times, the force of this objection will entirely be removed. His sleeping on the bare ground, for instance, with a stone for a pillow, was no extraordinary mortification for a monk, when the luxury of the rich could afford perhaps but a little straw. Besides, it was prudent for him to inure himself from choice to those habits of life at home, to which he must have generally submitted from necessity when he traveled abroad. The life of Columba was indeed mortified and self-denied, but had in it nothing irrational or unmeaning, nothing that looked like superstitious penance, or tormenting himself with unmeaning hardships. Accordingly, one of his biographers observes, that notwithstanding his austere and toilsome life, by which he was much spent and extenuated, yet he was comely in his dress and outward appearance, of a florid countenance and cheerful aspect; insomuch that he looked like one who lived in a nice and delicate manner.

Useless and ostentatious austerity he avoided himself and disliked in others. Hence, we find him sharply reproving a person who, by way of doing penance, affected to impose upon himself hardships which neither God nor his spiritual guides required. It was the practice of some saints, especially of Britain and Ireland, who used to subdue the body with the rigors of cold, by praying at night in the midst of ice and snow, and even immersed to the neck in cold water. This fashion, which never prevailed much, has passed away. But it may serve to make us think how little we do, for what others did so much. If they erred on one extreme, let us take care that we do not err upon another, which is more dangerous. St. Columba looked upon every part of religion as a pleasure and practiced it from choice, not as an imposed task or burden. No wonder then if it filled his heart with joy, and his countenance with gladness, for this is always its genuine effect on everyone who rightly understands its doctrines and sincerely obeys its precepts. This is, besides, the most effectual means to recommend our holy religion to others who are yet strangers to its power. Yes, cheerfulness is indeed the beauty of holiness, and contributed no doubt to Columba's acceptableness and usefulness, in conjunction with his affability, tenderness, and lowliness of mind. For lowliness of mind or humility shone in the character of Columba as much as any other quality, though he did not at any time affect or make a show of it. It is noted that Queen Margaret and King David of Scotland used to wash the feet of six beggars every night to exercise and show their humility, not considering that if the proud or evil spirit thus went out of one, he must have entered into six.

He was not only easy of access to all who came for either charity or instruction, as also affable and cheerful as became one who was filled with so much inward joy, but so humble as to condescend to the meanest service by which he could do good, and to take a share in grinding the corn, and other manual labor of the monks. The preference to which he was entitled he never assumed, being always disposed to think less highly of himself than of others. The greatest saints are always the most humble, a truth of which this man is an instance, although he had more temptation to pride than most men of his own or any other age. Courted, visited, and loved by all the petty kings and princes of Scotland and Ireland, revered and almost adored by the great body of their people, who crowded the roads where he traveled and brought their gifts to entertain him where he lodged. Obeyed by armies of monks in both kingdoms, and his company sought after by their bishops and abbots, who, without any mark of envy or emulation, acknowledged his vastly superior merit. What fuel was this to inflame his pride, if the last spark of it had not been quite extinguished! But we find Columba the same meek and lowly man to the very last, and so little uplifted with all the honors that could be done to him, that upon an occasion on which a whole country poured out to meet him, and surrounded him with hymns of joy and songs of gladness, his whole attention is taken up with a poor boy, whom he had singled out of the crowd on account of something in him which he thought a promising sign of piety and future usefulness. On what might glorify God or benefit man his thoughts were intent, and not on the glare of the triumph.

Of modesty, a virtue near akin to humility, Columba's biographers frequently observe that he had an uncommon share. The Office for his Festival says that virgin-modesty was one of the particular graces given him by God. Odonnellus says that his modesty was such that he could hardly look at any woman directly in the face. Nor is it improper to observe that this modesty is remarked to have been one of the guards by which the avenue of the eyes was defended against the entrance of any illicit thought that might infect his pure mind. For without strictly guarding the avenues of the senses, even saints ought not to presume on being secure from temptation. Columba, zealous of angelic purity and evangelic perfection, watched these doors with diligence; that nothing might enter in to hurt himself nor so much as an idle word come out to hurt another. Perhaps some may think his caution was excessive, and that his vigilance and labor both were more than were necessary. His own answer to some who told him so was, "For every idle word we have an account to render." He who does not strive shall never be crowned, he who does not run shall never win the race. To enter heaven requires all our exertion, and can never be expected by the secure and indolent.

From spiritual pride Columba was so free, that he avoided mentioning any of those special vouchsafements which were made to his soul. If the importunity of any who chanced to discover the effects of them, extorted from him a reluctant account of them, it was under promise or oath that as long as he lived they should say nothing of the matter. And though no man was more instant or earnest in prayer he is ready to ascribe the favors which he receives, not so much to his own prayers for them, as to the prayers of others. How amiable is such humility and how well-becoming every follower, and especially every minister, of the meek and lowly Jesus! And how incompatible is pride with their office, and with their usefulness.

With pride, or even pomp and magnificence in any clergyman, Columba had no patience; nor could he see it without being moved with indignation and denouncing its downfall. Observing one day a man driving his carriage along the plain of Bres, in much state, and only intent on his amusements, he asked who he was, and being told he was a rich clergyman he replied, "He may be so now, and enjoy his amusement and pleasure, but he is a poor man, indeed, on the day on which he dies." To see a clergyman depart from the gravity and sanctity of his character, or pass in diversion and idleness the time that should be devoted to the duties of his calling, is what Columba, with all his meekness, could never bear.

After so large an account of Columba's life and character, it may be expected that something should be said of his doctrine. A man of so much concern for the souls of men, we should naturally suppose would be faithful in declaring to them the whole counsel of God. For this his early education, and unwearied perseverance in study, rendered him peculiarly qualified. His passion for studying the scriptures especially was most intense, when the other parts of ministerial duty allowed him to indulge it. Thus we find him sometimes engaged for whole days and nights in exploring dark and difficult passages of scripture, and accompanying his study and application with prayer and fasting.

Hence Columba, and his disciples, for several generations, had a clearer and better knowledge of the gospel than most of their contemporaries, and taught it to the people in its native purity and simplicity. With the errors which at that time prevailed in the Church of Rome they seemed not to have been in the least tainted. Columba, instead of submitting to the spiritual tyranny of that church, withstood her errors, borrowed his monastic institutions from some Eastern churches, and declared that only to be the counsel of God in which he found the scriptures. Mr. Pinkerton justly observes that till the end of the 9th century, Iona was the Rome of Scotland, and we may add of at least a great part of Ireland. That Columba should have kept clear of the errors which prevailed in his time is the more remarkable. Odonellus says he visited Rome in person, which may be also implied in the Office for his Festival, in which he is celebrated for having visited distant places and of these the chief at the time was Rome. It was by proofs produced only from them; that his conduct was directed and his doctrine confirmed. The venerable Bede, with all his zeal for the Church of Rome, allows the divines of Hi (or Iona) to have possessed at the highest knowledge of divinity, and acknowledge how much the churches throughout Britain were indebted to them, for their preaching the gospel so zealously and accompanying it with such purity and simplicity of manners. At the same time he laments how long they wanted the only thing which, in his opinion, they needed in order to be perfect-the rites of the church-especially the right knowledge of Pasch and Tonsure. How the missionaries from Iona were qualified to preach the gospel (as Bede tells us) to the Saxons, or people of England, who had a different language, is a matter that requires to be explained, and points out, perhaps, a method which in such cases deserves to be imitated. To accomplish their object, they brought some Saxons to Iona, from whom they might learn the language of the country to which they were going, as well as educate them for returning, when fit for it, to teach their countrymen. Thus we find Adomnan mentions several Saxons in Iona, such as St. Pilo, a Saxon; St. Gueren, a Saxon; and a Saxon baker.

If St. Passadius and St. Patrick, who preached the gospel in Ireland before St. Columba, were sent by the Pope of Rome, as many authors affirm, it is probable that Columba may have differed in some points from those who taught before him. For this difference of opinion, which might lead him to reject the traditions and usurpations of man, it was perhaps owing that he ran the hazard of being excommunicated before he left Ireland, notwithstanding the holiness of his life, which his opponents themselves confessed to have shone as a light from heaven. Adomnan does not mention the cause, but calls it trivial, and Odonellus gives the following account of it, which is perhaps more curious than satisfactory. Columba being on a visit to St. Finnen, got a book from him to read, with which he was so much pleased that he sat up for some nights to take a copy of it. When he had done, Finnen would not allow him allow him to take with him, but insisted on having the copy returned along with the original. To avoid any dispute both agreed to refer the matter to Dermit King of Ireland; who decided in favor of Finnen, in the following words, which have since become proverbial, "To every cow belongs its calf, to every book belongs its copy." Soon after, a war having broke out between Dermit and the king or prince of Connaught, the former was worsted, and a great many of his people slain, in the battle of Culdremin A.D. 561. As the leaders of the Connaught party were the near relations of Columba, the victory was ascribed to his supposed prayers in their behalf, which excited against him the general indignation of the king and clergy on the other side. To avoid which, it is said, he immediately resolved, with the advice of St. Mael-Jos, to leave the kingdom. As we do not find Columba's influence was lessened in Ireland, the true cause of his leaving it must have been his zeal to extend his usefulness.

This intended indignity, however, was soon compensated by the veneration paid him by all ranks of people, there as well as in other kingdoms. It is a curious fact in history, though not so generally known as it deserves, that a large body of pastors and people in the isles and mountains of Scotland, like the Waldenses among the Alps, maintained the worship of God in its simplicity, and the gospel in its purity for many generations when it was greatly corrupted in other places. In the early ages of the Christian church, the Highlands and Islands of Scotland were the seat of learning and religion. Religion that was not derived from the Church of Rome, as appears from their differing from it about the time of keeping Easter and several other things. Icolmkill was then a seminary of all kinds of learning, and a nursery of divines for planting churches. In England, with great zeal, many of them taught and propagated religion out of the prophetic and apostolic writings. As noted by Bonar, "In some of our islands which we are now apt to consider as the seats of ignorance and barbarism, lived a people remarkable for simplicity of manners, purity of behavior, and unaffected piety; and these were the little leaven which afterwards leavened the whole lump. Of their numbers was Columba. Even in the 10th age, when the darkness of corruption and error had greatly increased, we are told there were some godly men in Scotland, who taught the true doctrine of Christ's atonement, and continued to exercise their functions apart, without acknowledging the authority of those who assumed a spiritual power over God's heritage."

But we return to Columba, and observe that although he did not at any time depart from the purity of scripture, he seems to have been at great pains to dress its doctrines in such a form as was most likely to engage the attention of a people who, like all uncivilized nations, were much more accustomed to indulge their imagination than to exercise their judgement. Several instances of his thus dexterously accommodating his representations of Divine truths to the circumstances and capacities of his hearers, may be observed in the account of his life by Adomnan. The monks, for instance, in the first period of their institution, had uncommon trials to encounter, and were to exhibit to the world a higher degree of sanctity and mortification than other men. They, therefore, were to be cheered with higher rewards and brighter prospects. The saints shall rise first, was a text which naturally suggested a prior resurrection to the monks, to whom the appellation of saints was more peculiarly, though not exclusively, appropriated, and to have a share in their resurrection was the first object of ambition and the promise of it a source of special consolation. Besides this, as many were in those barbarous times called forth to suffer and to die for the cause of God, and needed every help to make them encounter any form of death with cheerfulness, the innocent expedient was devised of assigning to the martyrs a separate burying place where their sacred dust was never to be contaminated with that of ordinary men. To sleep in this holy of holies, still known by the name of the Martyr's Cemetery, was to saints themselves an object of desire.

We know that angels conduct the spirits of the just to heaven; and Satan being prince of the power of the air, their way must be through his dominion; so that a conflict between two such opposite powers may naturally be supposed. In the sculpture on the pillars of the cathedral of Iona, is still to be seen the representation of Michael and the Devil weighing souls in a balance. By an obvious and lively figure of speech an animated preacher might, on the death of an acquaintance, represent this conflict as if he saw it, and describe its probable issue, suitably to the character of the departed, especially if it was decidedly marked as very good or very bad. Columba, whose fancy was lively, sometimes sat thus in judgement on the dead, in order to excite the living to virtue.

When saints, after so many intervening dangers, were thus brought safe to heaven, it was natural for the church on earth to celebrate the triumph and to rejoice at the happy transit and deliverance of a departed member of their body. Accordingly, on such occasions, Columba convened his monks, sang hymns, administered the Eucharist, and praised God for His mercy to the soul of a brother. On a certain day, as the brethren were making ready in the morning to go out to the different works in which they were to be employed, Columba told them they were to keep that day as a holiday. They should prepare for celebrating the Eucharist, and make some addition to their little dinner, as on the Lord's Day, out of respect for the soul of St. Columban, bishop of Leinster, whose soul was last night carried by choirs of angels to the paradise of God beyond the starry heavens. And if his life was remarkable for sanctity and usefulness, this, as it were his birthday, was for the future observed as a holiday as oft as the year returned. This custom, which in those times was pretty general, had the strongest tendency to promote holiness of life, and to make the virtuous look forward with joy to the day on which they were to have the happiness of dying.

As angels are ministering spirits, and the saints said to be after death as angels, so Columba represented the departed saints as being tenderly concerned for their surviving friends and employed to perform the office of angels to their souls, at the time of their departure from the body. "Happy happy woman," said Columba, on the occasion of the death of a pious woman, "this moment the angels convey thy soul to paradise!" Next year her husband, who was equally pious, died also,"What joy must it give him now at his departure," said Columba, "to be met by the soul of his wife, together with holy angels, to bring him to the mansions of the blessed!" Death, attended with the lively belief of such pleasing circumstances, had in it little to be feared. These examples, as well as the doctrine of those holy men, helped to strip death of its terrors and to make it more than welcome to the beholders. A country man who had come to see St. Aed on his death bed was so struck with what he saw and heard, that he immediately threw himself into the same bed, where he lay with the saint, till both died together.

As Columba himself rejoiced at the prospect of death, so also did his disciples. St. Odhran, one of the twelve who first accompanied him from Ireland, finding himself unwell soon after he landed, expressed his desire that his soul might be soon with Christ, and his body the first pledge that should consecrate Iona to his companions. "My dear Odhran," said Columba, "shall have both his wishes, and they who

Interior of St. Oran's Chapel, prepared for Divine Liturgy

shall hereafter ask for my tomb, shall next inquire, Where is Oran's?" Accordingly, Relic Orain is still shown to strangers.

Sometimes we find Columba teaching by actions instead of words. As he and Baithen had been walking on the shore, they saw a boat sinking, by which several persons perished. After lamenting their fate, and observing that one of them was very wicked, Baithen asked how God allowed the innocent to be sometimes involved in the punishment of the wicked? Of this Columba seemed to take no notice till they came to a beehive, in examining which, one of the bees stung Baithen, upon which, with a sweep of his hand, he killed it with several more. Why, said his master, did you kill the innocent with the guilty? I suppose it is because they were in bad company. Columba embraced every opportunity of turning every incident to the purpose of edification. Odonell says "There is a poor woman gathering wild herbs for food. Are we not ashamed to see some take more pains to preserve a perishing life, than we do to obtain that which is eternal?" From these instances we may easily perceive that Columba was at great pains to prepare and suit his manner of teaching to the exigencies and capacity of his hearers, by giving spiritual doctrines as it were, a body and a local habitation. And it deserves our notice, that after all his pains and preparation, he was so sensible that his sufficiency was not of himself. He seems to dread the discharge of the ordinary part of his public functions without previous prayer for the Divine assistance. Before he administers the ordinance of baptism, we find him retiring first to a private place to pray.

Having this high sense of the importance of his public ministrations, it is no wonder that he performed them with animation and sensibility. From this, his warm and affecting manner, and from the extraordinary alacrity and joy with which he discharged every part of his duty, may have proceeded, in part at least, those wonderful accounts already mentioned of the irradiation of his countenance. It shone on some occasions, with a glorious and heavenly luster, when he was engaged in the celebration of the holy ordinances of religion. This by those who are unwilling ascribe it (with Cumin and Adomnan) to the presence and manifestations of angels.

After having discharged the ordinary functions of his office, he had then also the same earnestness of soul, and the same solicitous concern for the success of his ministry. Thus, we have remarked that prayers to God for prospering his labors occupied the thoughts of his heart when asleep as well as when awake so entirely was his soul engaged in accomplishing the salvation of immortal spirits. Having given this account of the life and doctrine of Columba, we now turn our eye to the close of his long and useful life, as we have it in the relation of Adomnan.

He had some time ago told that the prayers of the churches had added four years to the appointed number of his days. During the last of these years he also dropped several hints to his monks of his beginning to die in the course of it, that he might thence take occasion to furnish them with proper consolation, and fortify and prepare them against that mournful event. One day particularly, in the month of May, being unable to walk as far as the west end of the island where the monks were at work, he went thither in a little car, or carriage, as he told, for the last time. He expressed his satisfaction that his death, which was now near, had not interfered with the Paschal solemnity and dampened their festivity, and seeing them greatly affected with this hint of his dear departure, he gave them all the consolation in his power before he left them. After this, having all the island before him to the east, he solemnly implored the blessing of God upon the ground, and upon all its inhabitants, adding, that it would go well with them while they feared God. It was on this occasion that Columba prayed (as St. Patrick is said to have done in regard to Ireland) that, while the people of Iona feared God, there should not be from that day forward any serpent or venomous creature in the island to hurt man or beast. On the ensuing Sabbath, while, according to his custom on the Lord's Day, he was celebrating the solemnity of mass, his countenance suddenly was observed to glow and color and to give symptoms of some unusual and ecstatic joy which he then felt. Concerning which he afterwards told some of those present, when they asked the cause, that he had seen the Angel of the Lord come to bring to God some deposit precious in His sight, but did not mention particularly what it was.

In eight days after this, in the course of the Sabbath, he went out along with his servant Dermit, and entering the barn, where he saw two heaps of corn, he expressed great satisfaction and thanked God, whose bounty had thus provided a sufficiency of bread for his dear monks on this year on which he was to leave them. During this year, said Dermit wiping his eyes, you have often made us all sad by the mention of your death. Yes Dermit, replied the saint, but I will now be more explicit with you, on condition that you promise to keep what I tell you a secret till I die; that there may be no bustle on that occasion about me. Dermit promised to do so, and thus the saint went on, "This day, in the sacred volume, is called the Sabbath, that is rest, and will be indeed a Sabbath to me; for it is to me the last day of this toilsome life. The day on which I am to rest from all my labor and trouble, for on this sacred night of the Lord, at the midnight hour, I go the way of my fathers. So my gracious Lord hath vouchsafed to intimate, and all my desire and joy is to be with Him."

Dermit wept bitterly, and the saint administered to him all the consolation in his power. After a little time, Dermit, being somewhat composed, they left the barn and the saint, resting a little on the way, that tender incident occurred which had been already mentioned. He afterwards ascended a little eminence above his monastery, where he stood, and lifting both his hands to heaven, prayed God to bless it and to make it prosper. From thence he returned to his closet, and having spent part of his time there in transcribing the Psalter, came to that passage in the 34th Psalm where it is said, "They that seek the Lord shall not want any good thing." He said, "Here I have come to the end of a page, and to a very proper part for me to stop at; for the following words (Come, ye children, hearken unto me; I will teach you the fear of the Lord) will better suit my successor than me. I will therefore leave it to Baithen to transcribe them." He then rose, and went to evening service in the church, and after coming home, sat down on his bed, and gave it in charge to Dermit to deliver the following words to his disciples as his last. "My dying charge to you, my dear children, is that you live in peace, and sincerely love one another. And if you do this, as becometh saints, the God who comforts and upholds the good will help you; and I, now that I am going to dwell with Him, will request that you may have both a sufficient supply of the necessaries of the present transitory life, and a share in that everlasting bliss which he has prepared for those who observe his holy laws."

After this he rested or remained silent, till the bell was rung for vigils at midnight, when, hastily rising and going to church, he arrived there before any other, and kneeled down at the altar to pray. When Dermit, who did not walk or rather run so hard, approached the church, he perceived it (as did also those who followed him) all illumined, and, as it were, filled with a heavenly glory or angelic light which, on his entering the door, immediately vanished. Upon which Dermit cried with a lamentable voice, "O my father, where art thou! My father, where art thou!" And groping, without waiting for the lamps, he found the saint lying before the altar in a praying posture. Dermit, attempting to raise him up a little, sat beside him, supporting the saint's head upon his bosom till the lights came in when the brethren, seeing their father dying, raised all at once a most doleful cry. Upon this the saint, whose soul had not yet departed, lifted up his eyes, and looked around him with inexpressible cheerfulness and joy of countenance, seeing no doubt the holy angels who were come to meet his spirit. He then attempted, with Dermit's assistance, to raise his right hand to bless the monks who were about him, and his voice, having failed, he made, with his hand alone, the motion which he used in giving his benediction. After which he immediately breathed out his spirit but still retained the tranquil smile, the brightness, and the fresh look of his countenance, so that he had the appearance not of one who was dead, but only sleeping.

After the spirit had departed, says Adomnan, when the morning hymns were ended, the sacred body was carried from the church to the house by the brethren, amidst the loud singing of psalms, and

A representation of the stained glass panel of St. Columba, located at Iona Abbey museum

An original standing cross of Iona

kept for three days and three nights, which were spent in the sweet praises of God. The venerable body of our holy and blessed patron, wrapped in fair linen sheets, and put in a coffin prepared for him, was then buried with all due respect, to rise in luminous and eternal glory on the day of the resurrection.

Adomnan gives a beautiful and classical description of two other extraordinary visions, which, he says, had been seen on the night on which Columba died. One of them by a holy man in Ireland (Lugud Mac Talcain) who had told next morning that Columba was dead; and the other by a number of fishermen who had been that night fishing in Glen Fende, from some of whom Adomnan had the relation when a boy. The purport of both is, that on the night and hour on which Columba, the pillar of so many churches, had departed, a pillar of fire which illumined the sky with a light brighter than that of the midday sun, was seen to arise from Iona, while loud and sweet sounding anthems of innumerable choirs of angels ascending with his soul were distinctly heard. And that when this column reached the heavens, the darkness again returned, as if the sun had suddenly set at noon.

Such lively pictures of the opinions of former times will not displease the antiquary, nor appear insignificant to the good and pious man. The cold skeptic may perhaps smile at the credulity of former ages; but credulity is more favorable to the happiness of man, and to the interests of society. Shall we then refuse all credit to human testimony, or shall we allow that a kind Providence may have adapted itself to the dark state of society, and given such visible and striking proofs of the connection and communication between this world and a world of spirits, as may be properly withheld from more enlightened times which may less need them, and perhaps less deserve them? Adomnan says that even in his time, a heavenly light and manifestation of angels was frequently seen at Columba's tomb.

Thus on the 9th day of June, 597, and in the 77th year of his age, died Columba, a man whose extraordinary piety, parts, and usefulness, accompanied with a perpetual serenity of mind, cheerfulness of countenance, simplicity of manners, benevolence of heart, and sweetness of disposition, have deservedly raised to the first rank of saints or holy men. The contemplation of his life and character may teach all, in every situation, and especially those in the sacred office, this useful and important lesson. That we have in us a capacity, if exerted, of attaining, by the grace of God, to such measures both of holiness and usefulness, as we are little aware of unless we make a fair trial. And without such a trial it is to no purpose that we see in the lives of holy men how good we may be ourselves, and what good we may do to others. These two points are the sum of all that has been advanced in the account which we have given of the life of Columba.

Such was the close of our venerable patron's life, who is now, according to the Scriptures, associated to Patriarchs, Prophets, and Apostles, and to those thousands of saints who are clothed in white robes, washed in the blood of the Lamb, and who follow Him withersoever he goeth. Such was the grace vouchsafed to his pure and spotless soul by Jesus Christ our Lord, to whom with the Father and the Holy Spirit, be honor and power and praise and glory and eternal dominion forever and ever. Amen!

APPENDIX

After Columba's death, an account of his life was written by many of his friends and disciples. Nine of these are enumerated by Dempster, and the list is increased to fifteen by Colgan. None of their writings are now extant, except those of Cumin and Adomnan. But five or six more of them are frequently quoted by Magnus Odonellus (a prince or nobleman of Tirconnel) who, in the year 1520, compiled a long account of the life of St Columba, from such monuments as were then extant. This account, which was written in the Irish language, was afterwards abridged and translated into Latin, by J. Colgan, an Irish friar who published it in 1647 in his Trias Thaumaturga.

Of Columba's own writings, of which Odonellus says there were a "great many, full of piety and devotion, some in prose, but mostly in Latin or Irish verse," there are now but very few remaining. St. Evin, who wrote a life of St. Patrick in the sixth century, mentions Columba as having wrote a life of that saint (Vita Tripart, S. Pat). Wilifred, the author of the life of St. Ciaran and Alcuin, mention his having composed a monastic rule which Ware says was extant in his time. He also composed a rule for hermits of which Colgan says he had a copy in his possession. He also wrote a number of hymns and poems, both in Irish and Latin, as already mentioned. Ten of the Irish poems were in the possession of Colgan, who gives the title and first line of each of them. Of these, which are probably still extant in Ireland, I have seen none but his Farewell to the Monastery of Durrough.

Of Columba's Latin hymns or poems, Colgan has published three. One of them was composed during a thunderstorm in Durrough, or Daire-Chalguich; another of them on the creation, fall of angels, and final judgement, and the third, addressed to the Redeemer, was composed, it is said, in consequence of an observation made to him that the Redeemer ought to have been more celebrated in the proceeding hymn.

As Columba intended that his disciples should commit these hymns to memory, they are composed in a sort of rhyme, agreeably to the form and measure of Irish poetry, to which they were so much accustomed. In their Latin form they may appear somewhat irregular to those not acquainted with the rules of Irish poetry, but the English version, presented here, these translations will show the nature of the original.

HYMN

Completed during a thunderstorm about the year 550

Gracious Father I bow Thine ear
And our request in mercy hear:

O bid the thunder cease to roar,
And let the lighting flash no more;
Left long in terror we remain,
Or by its stroke we should be slain.

The power supreme to Thee belongs,
Archangels laud Thee in their songs;
The wide expanse of heaven above,
Resounds Thy glory and Thy love.

O Savior of the human race!
Whose power is equal to Thy grace;
For ever be thy name adored,
As King supreme, and only Lord!
To all Thy people Thou art nigh,
And oft Thy grace prevents their cry;
While in the womb the Baptist lay
(The harbinger to pave the way),
His soul with grace was amply stored,
To fit him to proclaim his Lord.

May love and zeal to Thee, my God!
Have in my heart a firm abode:
O that the casket may be such
As fits a gem so very rich!

Stormy skies off the coast of Iona

HYMN II

On the Creation, Fall of Angels, Final Judgement...

The God omnipotent, who made the world,
Is subject to no change. He was, He is,
And He shall be: ETERNAL is His name.

Equal in godhead and eternal power
Is Christ the Son. So is the Holy Ghost.
These sacred glorious three are but the same;
In persons different, but one God and Lord.

This God created all the heavenly hosts;
Archangels, angels, potentates and powers;
That so the emanations of His love
Might flow to myriads, diffusing good.

But from this eminence of glory fell
The apostate Lucifer, elate with pride
Of his high station and his glorious form.
Filled with like pride, and envying God Himself
His glory, other angels shared his fate,
While the remainder kept their happy state.

Thus fell a third of the bright heavenly stars,
Involved in the old serpent's guilt and fate,
And with him suffer in the infernal gulf
The loss of heaven, in chains of darkness bound.

God then to being called this lower world,
According to the plan formed in His mind.
He made the firmament, the earth, and sea,
The sun, the moon and stars; a glorious host!
The earth He clad with herbs for food, and trees,

And then to every living things gave birth,
And last to man, whom he made lord of all.

When angels (the first morning stars) beheld
The wondrous fabric, with glad songs they hymned
The praise of the Almighty architect,
For such displays of wisdom, power, and love.

But our first parents, from their happy state
Seduced by Satan, were with terror filled,
With dreadful sights appalled, till God with grace
Consoled their hearts, and Satan's power restrained
His providential care he also showed,
And bade the humid clouds distil their rains,
And times and seasons in their order run.
Rivers and seas (like giants bound in chains)
He forced to keep within the limits fixed,
And flow forever for the use of man.

Lo! Earth's vast globe, suspended by His power,
On nothing hands, as on a solid base.
Hell, too, His word obeys; where monsters dire,
And flames, and fire, and smoke, and gnawing worms,
Torment His foes, who gnash their teeth with pain.
Though once they slighted, now they feel His power,
And must reluctantly His will obey.

O happy they who love His holy law,
And in the blessings of the saints partake!
Who in the paradise of God above
Drink of the living stream, and eat the fruit
Of that life-giving tree, ordained by God
To heal the nations, and to feed the soul.

Thrice happy is the soul that shall ascend
To this abode of God, when the last trump
Shall sound, and shake the earth more than of old,
When Sinai shook, and Moses was afraid.

This awful day of God the Lord draws nigh,
When earthly objects shall have lost their charm,
And joy or terror fill each human soul.
Then shall we stand before the judgement seat,
To render an account of all our deeds;
Then shall our sins before our face be set,
The books be opened, and the conscience heard.
None shall be missing; for the dead shall hear
The voice of God, and from their graves come forth
To join their souls, and stand before the bar.

Time runs his course no more: the wandering orbs
Through heaven lose their course: the sun grows dark,
Eclipsed by the glory of the Judge.
The stars drop down, as in a tempest, fruit
Is shaken from the tree: and all the earth,
Like one vast furnace, is involved in flames.
See! The angelic hosts attend the Judge,
And on ten thousand harps His praises hymn.
Their crowns they cast before His feet, and sing,
"Worthy the Lamb that died to be the Judge!
"To Father, Son, and Holy Ghost, be praise!"

The sentence past, consuming fire shall seize
The unbelieving, disobedient crowd:
But we who have believed, and kept His word,
Shall enter into glory with the Lord;
And there, in different ranks, we shall receive,
Through grace, rewards proportioned to our deeds,

And dwell in endless glory with our Lord.

Almighty Father, Son, and Holy Ghost,
Thou one eternal, ever-blessed God!
To me, the least of saints, vouchsafe Thy grace!
O may I join the thousands round Thy throne!

HYMN III

To the Redeemer

Jesus! May all who trust in Thee
Experience Thy love:
That Thou art God forevermore
By their salvation prove.

In time of trouble and distress
Be Thou their faithful friend;
In all their sorrows comfort them,
And ready succor send.

Thou art the Father of the just,
Their souls have life in Thee;
Thou art their God omnipotent,
And evermore shalt be.

The world, with all that it contains,
From Thee its being had;
O'er all the nations Thou wilt rule,
And judge the quick and dead.

Thy glory shines above the skies,
Where Thou art God and King;

And to the New Jerusalem
Thy people thou wilt bring.

Eternal God! Who can conceive
Thy power or Thy grace?
Through endless ages they endure,
And fill the bounds of space.

The Father, Son, and Holy Ghost,
While I have life I'll praise;
And after death, in other worlds,
The song again I'll raise.

Gracious Savior of the world:
The pure are Thy delight;
O give me wisdom from above
To guide me in the right.

Defend me by Thy mighty power,
Until my warfare's over,
And with the martyrs afterwards
May I Thy name adore.

As Thou didst suffer on the cross
To save a guilty race,
Show me Thy power, with Thy love,
And glory grant, with grace.

Eternal praise to the Most High,
The Father and the Son,
And to the Spirit of all grace,
The eternal Holy One.

Protect us, O Thou God most high,

Until we reach the place
Where endless anthems we shall sing
Around Thy throne of grace.

Another poem or epistle, against avarice, in appropriate Latin verse, is preserved by Canisius, who is disposed to ascribe it to the other St. Columba or Columbanus, the countryman and contemporary of this. It is not unworthy of either, and may be read as one of the monuments of the learning of the times, without determining to which of the two it belongs. The following version will give an idea of it to the English reader.

Epistle to Hunald Against Avarice
Hunald! The Counsel of Columba Hear,

And to thy friend give now a willing ear;
No studied ornament shall gild my speech,
What love shall dictate, I will plainly preach.

Have faith in God, and His commandments obey,
While fleeting life allows you here to stay;
And know, the end for which this life is given,
Is to prepare the soul for God and heaven.
Despite the pleasures which will not remain,
Nor set thy heart on momentary gain:
But seek for treasures in the sacred page,
And in the precepts of each saint and sage.
These noble treasures will remain behind
When earthly treasures fly on wings of wind.

Think of the time when trembling age shall come,

And the last messenger to call thee home.
'Tis wise to meditate betimes on death,
And that dread moment which will stop the breath,
On all the ills which age brings in its train,
Disease and weakness, languor, grief and pain.
The joints grow stiff, the blood itself runs cold,
Nor can the staff its trembling load uphold.
And need I speak of groans and pangs of mind,
And sleep disturbed by every breath of wind?
What then avails the heap of yellow gold,
For years collected, and each day re-told?
Or what avails the table richly stored
To the sick palate of its dying lord?
The sinful pleasures which have long since past,
Are now like arrows in his heart stuck fast.

He who reflects that Time, on eagle-wing,
Flies past, and preys on every earthly thing,
Will scorn vain honors, avarice despise,
On nobler pursuits bent, beyond the skies.

Alas! Vain mortals, how misplaced your care,
When in this world you seek what is not there?
True lasting happiness is found above,
And heaven not earth, you therefore ought to love.
The rich enjoy not what they seem to have,
But something more their souls incessant crave.
The use of riches seldom do they know;
For heirs they heap them, or they waste in show.

O! Happy he, to whose contented mind
Riches seems useless, but to help mankind;
Who neither squanders what should feed the poor,
Nor suffers Avarice to lock his store.

No moths upon his heaps of garments feed,
Nor serves his corn to feed the pampered steed.
No cankering care shall take his peace away;
No thief, nor flame, shall on his substance prey.
His treasure is secure beyond the skies,
And there he finds it on the day he dies.

This world we entered naked at our birth,
Naked we leave it, and return to earth:
Silver and gold we need not much, nor long;
Since to this world alone such things belong.
Life's little space requires no ample store:
Soon heaven opens to the pious poor;
While Pluto's realms their dreary gates unfold,
Those to admit who set their souls on gold.

Our Savior bids us Avarice avoid,
Nor love those things which can't be long enjoyed.
Short, says the Psalmist, are the days of man,
The measure of his life a narrow span.
Time flies away; and on its rapid wing
We fly along, with every earthly thing.
Yet Time returns, and crowns the Spring with flowers,
Renews he seasons, and repeats the hours.
But life returns not with revolving years,
And man, once gone, on earth no more appears.
Wise then is he who makes it his great care,
In this short space, for heaven to prepare.

From its connection with the subject, it may not be improper to add the following translation of a hymn used in the Office for the festival of St. Columba, and published in Paris, in the year 1620, from an ancient MS. It was probably composed by Baithen, or some other of Columba's disciples, soon after his death.

Translation of a Hymn used in the Office for the Festival of St. Columba, on the 9th of June

With snowy pinions soaring high,
The Dove ascends beyond the sky;
He scorns the earth, he leaves its clay,
And perches in the realms of day.

There his refulgent colors shine,
Reflecting back the light divine.
But here his tender brood he left,
Of their dear parent now bereft.

Yet, ere he mounted to the skies,
With many prayers, tears, and cries,
Their charge he gave to Christ his Lord,
To guide them by His gracious word,
And bring them to the same abode
In which their father lives with God.

O God! Who didst our father hear,
Be to his children ever near;
And grace vouchsafe to lead us on,
Until we meet him at Thy throne.

Attributed to St. Columba, written about Iona (ancient name I, Hi, or Aoi,

Latinized into Hyona and later I-colum-kill or The Isle of Colum of the Cells as included in one of the parishes of Mull) in prophecy of a time when the island will rise again from the ruins left by the Northmen.

O sacred dome, and my beloved abode!
Whose walls now echo to the praise of God;
The time shall come when lauding monks shall cease,
And lowing herds here occupy their place:
But better ages shall thereafter come,
And praise re-echo in this sacred dome.

Another Prayer Attributed to St. Columba

Let me bless almighty God,
Whose power extends over sea and land,
Whose angels watches over all-

Let me study sacred books to calm my soul,
I pray for peace,
Kneeling at Heaven's gates.

Let me do my daily work,
Gathering seaweed, catching fish,
Giving food to the poor.

Let me say my daily prayers,
Sometimes chanting, sometimes quiet,
Always thanking God.

Delightful it is to live,
On a peaceful isle, in a quiet cell-
Serving the King of Kings!

Ionian seaweed, likely the same species collected by the monks

OF THE MONASTERIES AND CHURCHES FOUNDED BY ST. COLUMBA

Jocelin says that Columkille founded 100 monasteries. Hanmer, Usher, and others say the same. Odonellus says that of monasteries and churches together he founded 300, partly in Ireland and partly in Scotland. The following is a list of the principal monasteries and churches founded by St. Columba in Ireland (of which the names of the first Abbots, and some other particulars, may be found in Colgan, and in the authors which he cites.)

> *Mon. of Doire-Chalguich, or Durrough, now Derry*
> *--of Darmagh (Roboreti campus. Ad.)*
> *Church of Rath-Reghenden, in the diocese of Derry*
> *Mon. of Kill-Aibhne, or Kill-Aibhind*
> *--of Snamh-Luthuir, in Connaught*
> *--of Drim-Tuam, in Tirconnel*
> *--of Tir-da-chraobh, al. mon. of the two rivers*
> *--of Drim-finchoil*
> *--of Sean-glean, in Tirconnel*

--of Gartan, in do
--of Tulach-Dubhglais, in do
--of Kill-mac-nenain, in do
--of Cluain, or Cluain-enaich, in the diocese of Derry
--of Rath-bo; long a bishop's see in Tirconnel
--of Drim-cliabh, in the north of Connaught
--of Kenannais, in Media, olim nobile
--of Clauain-mor-Fernard
--of Rechrain, in Parte Bregarum
--of Rechlain, island
--of Surd, olim nobile
--of Torrachan, an island, north of Tirconnel
--of Rath, in Tirconnel
--of Termonn Cethmanaich, in Tironia
--of S. Columba's Coffer, olim ditissmum, in Ardia
Mon. of Innis-loch-gamhna, in Connaught.
--of Eas-mac-neirc, in do
--of Imleach-foda, olim nobile
--of Druim-Choluim-cille, in Tir-oileail
--of Kill-mor-Dithreibh, in Connaught
--of Maoin-Cholum-chille, in Leinster
--of S. Columba's Coffer, in Media Orientali (often pillaged)
--of Cnoc-na Maoile, in Connaught
--of Kill-chuana, in do
--of All-Farannain, in do
--of S. Columba's Coffer (Scrinium S. Col.) in Tironia
--of Kill-lukin, in Connaught
--of Cluain-ogcormacain, in regione Siol-mhuir'ich
--of Kill-tuama, in Tir-maine, Connaught
--of Disert-Egnich, in Innis-owen
--of Cluain-maine, in do
Church of Kill-matoige, diocese Med
Mon. of Fathen-mura, in Innis-owen
--of Uisge-chaoin, diocese of Derry

--of Baile-mag-rabhartaich, in do
--of Teach-Bhaithen, in Tirconnel
--of Cluain-laoidh, in do
--of Both-medha, in Ulster
--of Tamlacht-Fionlugain, diocese of Derry
--of Disert-Hi Thuachuill, in do
--of Dun-bo, in do
--of Aregal, in do
--of Gleann-Choluim-chille, in Tuam
--of Kill-Cholgain, in Clonfert
--of Baile-megrabhartich, in Tir-Aodh (in which was kept Columba's book, called Cathach, from its being carried before the army in the field of battle)
--of Kill-bhairrind, in Tir-Aodh
--of Regles Choluim-chille, in Ardmagh

To these, says Colgan, may be added almost all the other churches in Tirconnel, many of those of Lower Connaught; and all the churches, of which we find his disciples had the charge, as Innis-cail, Innis Mhuiredhich, Port-Lomain, Teach-Earnain, etc.

Of the monasteries and churches founded by St. Columba in Scotland, no particular account can be given, as the records of them have not been preserved. We can only say in general, that he planted churches in all the Western Isles, and in all the territory of the ancient Scots and northern Picts, and some even beyond them. Colgan, and authors cited by him, say he founded the church of Dunkeld, the monastery of Inch-colm in the Forth, and the monastery of Govan on the Clyde. Adomnan, besides the chief monastery of Iona, mentions several more in the Western Isles; such as that of Achaluing, in Ethica; Himba, or Hinba, also known as Elen-naomh; also Kill-Diun, or Dimha, at Lochava (or Lochow). Most of our parishes still bear the names of his disciples, and tell their founder; and the vast number of places, whose names begin with Kill, shows how thick our churches were anciently planted; so that there is much reason to believe that the largest number ascribed to Columba is not above the mark.

The holy well found at Kilninian, or the Church of St. Ninian, on Mull. There is a similar holy well on Hinba dedicated to St. Columba

Providence smiled in a remarkable manner on his labors, and his successes were astonishing. It is no wonder that so extraordinary a man should have been so much revered while alive, and his memory so much respected after his death. Accordingly, he is styled by foreign, as well as by domestic writers, the Apostle of the Scots and Picts, the patron Saint of both, and the joint patron of Ireland. Though only an abbot, he had the singular privilege of exercising (as did his successors) a jurisdiction over all their bishops, being primate of all their churches. Notkerus Balbulus, who ranks Columba almost with the first apostles, calls him also "Primate of all the Irish bishops", which the author of the life of St. Farran says he was made at the great council of Drimkeat. His successors, the abbots of Iona, seem for a considerable time to have had the same pre-eminence in Ireland as well as in Scotland. The acts of a synod of the clergy of Ireland, at which Adomnan presided in 695, are called "The Canons of Adomnan" and in 925 Maolbride seems to have had equal authority, as may be inferred from the annals of the Quat. Magistri.

In after times, St. Columba was considered as the patron saint of the ancient Scots and Picts; and the patron saint of Ireland, in conjunction with St. Patrick and St. Bridget. To this honor, his merit in Ireland, as well as in Scotland, gave him the amplest title.

Both nations held him in such reverence that they thought their security depended upon their having his remains in their possession. The Pictish Chronicle says that Kenneth MacAlpin, after his conquest of the Picts, carried the relics of Columba to a church which he had built in his new territory. The Irish writers relate that they were carried to Ireland and placed in Down, in the same tomb with St. Patrick and St. Bridget. Giraldus Cambrensis says they were carried thither in 1185, by order of John de Curci, and repeats the well-known lines;

> *Hi tres in Duno, tumulo tumulantur in uno,*
> *Brigida, Patricius, atque Columba pius.*

These opinions and stories may serve to show the veneration which the people of both nations had for the memory and remains of Columba.

But the fame of Columba, and the veneration for his name, extended much farther than Britain and Ireland. Adomnan observes that "though Columba lived on a small, remote island of the British ocean, yet God had done him the honor to make his name renowned not only though all Britain and Ireland but through Spain, France, and Italy, particularly in Rome, the greatest city in the world. Thus, God honors those who honor Him; for which His holy name be praised."

Odonellus, who cites this passage from Adomnan, says in still stronger terms, that whilst the saint was yet alive almost all the countries

Lochbuie standing stones on Mull, a monument of Bronze Age paganism considered ancient in St. Columba's day

of Europe sounded with his fame. Several testimonies of foreign writers have been occasionally produced already to this purpose; to which I shall here add that of Anthony Yepez, who says, "About this time flourished the two Irish saints, of the name of Columbanus, or Columba; both of whom were so illustrious, that either of them would be alone sufficient to give celebrity to the whole nation to which they belonged. As they had the same name, so they had also the same generous zeal, and made the same noble exertions to spread the Gospel among heathen nations in foreign lands."

Of the Disciples of St. Columba

To the great success of Columba, the instruments employed under him must have contributed not a little. His disciples were men of learning, as well as of zeal and piety. He chose men of this stamp for his first associates; and his own seminaries furnished him afterwards with a sufficient supply of the same kind. Learning, when he set out in life, was in a very flourishing state in Ireland. In many of the lives of the Irish saints written in that age, we read of numerous schools, well attended, and taught by learned and aged masters; which could not have been the case, if as some maintain, letters had been introduced into the country no sooner than the time of St. Patrick. So general a diffusion of learning, and such acquaintance with the learned languages as Columba's masters and his contemporaries possessed, could not possibly have taken place in so short a period. But without entering further into this subject at present, it is enough to say that Columba found and chose men of learning, as well as of zeal and piety, to superintend his seminaries and to conduct his missions. He himself, with unwearied diligence, went through occasionally from province to province, through the whole of his immense diocese.

We had occasion to observe before, that he was at great pains to select the most promising youths and the children of pious parents for his disciples, and that the course of education and probation prescribed by him was very long; so that the learning, as well as the piety and prudence of every candidate was well proved before he was instructed with the cure of souls. We have seen a man, who thought himself already qualified for entering into orders, obliged by Columba to spend no less than seven years more in education and preparation before he could be ordained to the sacred office. Sanctity and zeal, when thus accompanied with learning, could not fail to make the disciples of Columba both respected and useful.

The instituting of schools and seminaries of learning, in which men were thus prepared for the ministry, and trained up from their infancy in the acts and habits of their office, and kept till their character was fully formed, and their qualifications well known and proved, had a powerful tendency to make their future labors successful. From his first monasteries in Ireland, Columba drew the necessary supplies till that over which he himself presided in Iona was in conditions to furnish as many as he needed. The excellency of his plan was sufficiently proved by the effect which it produced.

Another circumstance which greatly contributed to the success of Columba, especially in Ireland, was the high rank of many of his disciples. A great number of them were, like himself, of the family of Conal Gulbann, son of Niall Naoighealbach (or Neil of the Nine Hostages) monarch of Ireland. That country, long harassed by civil wars, listened gladly to a system which proposed peace on earth and which its effect upon those who first professed it, showed to be fully adequate to all that it proposed. Hence, many of the nobility not only embraced but preached the Gospel, and ranked themselves among the followers and disciples of Columba. It was then the fashion among great men to be great saints; a fashion which is long of coming round again, although one should think that self-preservation might now give the alarm and help to bring it about.

Among the circumstances which conducted to Columba's success may be mentioned the unusual length to which the lives of many holy men, who them preached the Gospel, were preserved. Their extreme temperance, constant exercise, and inward joy and serenity of mind would no doubt contribute to health and long life. But that the duration of it, accompanied with health and usefulness, should have been so long as we find from a variety of concurring testimonies can be ascribed only to the kind and particular providence of God being peculiarly concerned about their preservation. The age of St. Patrick, and some more, may probably be exaggerated. But it is pleasing to find the oldest of them represented as active and cheerful to the last, after all the toil of his daily duty.

Of Columba's own scholars or disciples, above one hundred had the honor of being sainted, and their festivals observed by the gratitude of those places which they benefited by their labors, as we find from the accounts given of them by various authors. The following noted are a list of contemporaries and disciples of St. Columba:

(The twelve who came with Columba at first to Iona are marked thus *)

St. Aidan, or Aodhan, son of Libher, afterwards Bishop of Lindisfarne

St. Aidan, son of Kein, Abbot of Cuil-uife.
(There are twenty seven saints of this name)

St. Ailbhe, son of Ronan

St. Aonghus, of Dermagh

St. Baithan, of Doire-chalguich

St. Baithen, son of Brendan, Abbot of Hi

St. Barrind, Abbot of Kill-barrind

St. Becan, son of Ernan, brother of Cumin Fionn

St. Bec, or Beg-bhile, son of Tighearnach

St. Berach, a monk of Hi, Abbot of Cluain-choirpe

St. Berchan, or Barchan

St. Bran, or Branni', in Doire-chalguich, nephew of Columba

St. Cailten, of Kill-Diun, or Dimha, at Loch-ava

*St. Carnan, son of Brandubh

*St. Ceata, or Catan, supposed by some to be the Bishop Ceadan of Bede; by others the Cetheus, surnamed Peregrinus, said by Herman. Greven, to have suffered martyrdom in Italy

St. Ceallach, Bishop of the Mercians, in England

St. Cobhran, son of Enan, nephew of Columba

*St. Cobhthach, son of Brendan, and brother of St. Baithen

St. Colgu, or Colgan, of Kill-cholgan, in Connaught

St. Colgan, son of Aodh Draighneach, a monk of Hi

St. Collan, of Dermagh

St. Colman, or Columan, founder of the monastery of Snamhluthir

St. Colman, Abbot of Hi, and afterwards of Lindisfarne

St. Colman, son of Comhgell, who died in 620

St. Colman, Abbot of Rechrain

St. Colman, son of Enan

St. Colman, son of Tighearnach, brother to Beg-bhile, Connan, and Cuan

St. Colman, son of Ronan

St. Colum Crag, of Enach in Ulster

St. Coman, or Comhan, brother to St. Cumin

St. Comgan, or Caomhghan, son of Deghille, and sister's son of Columba

St. Conall, Abbot of Innis-caoil, in Tirconnel

St. Conna, or Connan, surnamed Dil, son of Tighearnach

St. Conacht, son of Maoldraighneach

St. Conrach, Mac-Kein, of Dermagh Monastery

St. Constantin, or Cusandin, king of Cornubia, said by Fordun to have presided over the monastery of Govan upon Clyde, and to have converted the people of Kintyre, where he says he suffered martyrdom

St. Cormac Hua Liethain, Abbot of Darmagh

St. Corman, said to have been the first missionary to the Northumbrians, AD 630

St. Cuannan, Abbot of Kill-chuannain, in Connaught

St. Cuan, or Coan, son of Tighearnach

St. Cuchumin Mac-kein, Abbot of Hi

St. Cumin, surnamed Fionn, or Fair, Abbot of Hi, who wrote Columba's life

St. Dachonna, Abbot of Eas-mac-neirc

St. Dallan Forguill, formerly a bard or poet

St. Dermit, of the descendants of K. Leogaire

St. Dima, afterwards a Bishop of the Mercians in England

*St. Eochadh, or Eochadh Torannan

St. Enna, son of Nuadhan, Abbot of Imleachfoda, in Connaught

*St. Ernan, uncle to Columba, and Abbot of Hinba

St. Ernan, Abbot of Drim-tuam, in Tirconnel

St. Ernan, Abbot of Torrachan, of the race of King Niall

St. Ernan, of Teach-Ernain

Bishop Eoghan, or Eoghanan, a Pictish presbyter

St. Failbhe, Abbot of Hi

St. Farannan, Abbot of All-Farrannain, in Connaught

St. Fiachna, of Acha-luing, Ethica

St. Fechne, son of Rodan, 580 AD, martyred in Anglia

St. Fergna (Virgnous), Abbot of Hi

St. Finan, surnamed Lobhar, Abbot of Sourd, near Dublin

St. Finan, or Finthan, Abbot of Rath, in Tirconnel

St. Finan, or Fennin, Abbot of Magh-chofgain

St. Finan, an anchorite, supposed by some to be the same with the preceding

St. Finan, who succeeded Aidan as Bishop of Lindisfarne

St. Finbarr, Abbot of Drim-choluim, in Connaught

St. Finnchan, Abbot of Ardchaoin

St. Finnlugan, a monk of Hi

St. Finten, son of Aodh, founder of the Monastery of Caille-Abhind

Bishop Genere, or Gueren, a Saxon, or Anglo-Saxon

*St. Grellan, son of Rodan, or Grellan Aoibhleach

St. Hilary, or Elaire, son of Fintan, and brother of St. Aidan

St. Lasran, son of Feradach, Abbot of Darmagh

St. Lasran, called Hortulanus, or Gardener

St. Lasran, son of Deghille, and brother of St. Bran

St. Lasran, or Lasar, son of Ronan

St. Libhran, from Connaught

St. Loman, of Lochuair

St. Luga Ceanaladh, a monk of Hi

*St. Lugaide, of Cluain-laogh

St. Lugaid, Abbot of Cluain-Finchoil

St. Lugaid, surnamed Laidir, of Tir-da-chraobh

St. Lugbe Mac-cumin, a monk of Hi, Abbot of Elen-nao

St. Lugbe Mac-Blai', a monk of Hi

St. Lughne Mac-cumin, brother of St. Lugbe

St. Lughne Mac-Blai', brother of Lugbe Mac-Blai'

St. Mernoc, or Marnoc, of Cluain-reilgeach

St. Miril, sister's son of Columba

St. Maolchus, brother to St. Mernoc

St. Maoldubh, of Cluin-chonair

St. Maoldubh, son of Enan

St. Moab, or Abban, his brother

Bishop Maolcomha, son of Aodh Mac-Aimirleh, from a king became a monk

St. Maol-Odhrain, a monk of Hi

Bishop Maol-umha, son of Beothan, king of Ireland, a monk of Hi

St. Mochonna, son of Fiachna, King of Ulster, afterwards a Pictish bishop

*St. Mac-cuthen, said by Usher to have wrote a life of St. Patrick

St. Moulan, a monk of Hi

St. Moluoc, of the race of Conal Gulbann, Bishop of Lismore, died in 588

St. Mothorian, Abbot of Drim-cliabh

St. Munna, son of Tulchan, Abbot of Teach-mhunna

St. Pilo, an Anglo-Saxon, a monk of Hi

*St. Odhran, who died soon after he came to Hi, 27th October

St. Ossin, or Ossian, Abbot of Cluain-mor. There were several saints of this name. A poetical dialogue between one of this name and St. Patrick is still repeated, which Colgan observes could not have been composed by the son of Fingal, who lived long before.

*St. Rus, or Russien

*St. Scandal, son of Bresal, Abbot of Kil-chobhrain

St. Segin, son of Fiachri, Abbot of Hi

St. Segen, son of Ronan, Abbot of Bangor in 664

St. Senach, half-brother of Columba, Abbot of Doire-brosgaidh

St. Senan, a monk of Darmagh

St. Sillean, son of Neman, a monk of Hi

St. Suibhne, son of Curtre, Abbot of Hi

St. Ternoc, of Ari-molt, near Loch-Ern, Ulster

*St. Torannan, afterwards Abbot of Bangor, as Colgan thinks

St. Trenan Mac-Rintir, a monk of Hi

Bishop Tulchan, father of St. Munna and company, who followed his sons to Hi

Such as wish to know more of these saints, and others, may consult Colgan, Cathald, Maguir, Gorman, the Martyrologies of Dungallan, Tamlact, with the authors cited by them.

A BRIEF ACCOUNT OF IONA, AND OF COLUMBA'S SUCCESSORS

Before Columba died, he had got his chief seminary in Icolumkill or Iona put in such a state, that he was able to speak with confidence of its future glory and fame. His disciples accordingly supported its credit for many ages, and supplied not only their own, but other nations, with learned and pious teachers. "From this nest of Columba," says Odonellus, "these sacred doves took their flight to all quarters."

The other Columbanus, who after spending some time in the monastery of Bangor, passed from thence to France, afterwards to Germany, and at last to Italy, and "filled all those regions with monasteries" paved the way for them into all these countries, into which they poured in such numbers that both Ypez and St. Bernard compare them to hives of bees, or to a spreading flood. Wherever they went they disseminated learning and true religion, of both which they seem to have possessed the greatest share of any society then in Europe, and seem to have done more than any other towards the revival of both, when they were at their lowest ebb.

Foreign and Romish writers, accustomed to distinguish monks by their different orders, speak of the disciples of Columba in the same manner, and call them by different names, such as "Ordo Apostolicus" "Ordo Dini Columbae" "Congregatio Columbina" and "Ordo pulchrae societatis," but they themselves seem to have assumed no other name than that of Famuli Dei, or servants of God, or in their own language, Gille-De, which was Latinized into Keledeus, whence the English name of Culdees. These were generally formed into societies, consisting each of twelve and an abbot, after the example of their master, or of Christ and His Apostles, and their foreign missions were commonly conducted on a similar plan.

Iona continued to be the Archicenobium, or chief monastery, and its abbots the heads of all monasteries and congregations of the followers of Columba in Scotland and Ireland, for several ages, to which all its bishops were subject. The first check to its celebrity was the invasion of the Norwegians and Danes in the beginning of the ninth century. By them it was repeatedly pillaged and burnt, and its monks and abbots massacred. Soon after, it came to be under their settled dominion, together with the rest of the Western Isles. As those barbarians held learning in no estimation, the college of Iona, though it continued to exist, began to decline, and had its connection with Britain and Ireland in a great measure cut off. Dunkled affected then, for some time, to be the Primate's seat in Scotland, but did not long maintain its claim; for about the end of the 9th, or beginning of the 10th century, the legend of St. Regulus, and the apparition of St. Andrew, were invented; in consequence of which with the aid of King Grig, St. Andrew's came to be considered as the principle see of Scotland, and St. Andrew to be considered as the tutelar saint instead of St. Columba.

Still, however, the Culdees, or clergy of the order of Columba, retained their influence and respect, and often elected the bishops of their bounds. At length, in the 12th and 13th centuries, the Romish monks poured into the kingdom, supplanted by the Culdees, and by degrees got possession of all their monasteries. The followers of Columba, after their great and first concern of establishing Christianity in the kingdom was over, and religion fully settled, did not think it unlawful to marry and to take the charge of families as well as of the parishes. The new monks, on the other hand, lived in celibacy, affected greater purity and had more ceremony and show, so that the popular tide soon turned in their favor. The Culdees existed no longer in colleges, but for a long time after they continued to teach true Christianity apart so that the reign of error in these lands was very short, and the darkness of its night was intermixed with the light of many stars.

From these notices of Columba, and of his disciples, we may well apply to him in the beginning of his own ode to Ciaran.

> *A great apostle sent by God*
> *Hath blessed this isle with light,*
> *His beams, diffused through all the land,*
> *Dispelled the gloom of night.*

Iconic Iona

A Chronicle of Some Events Connected with the Monastery of Hi, or Iona, and Concurrent World History

A.D.

325 The First Council of Nicea

381 First Council of Constantinople

431 First Council of Ephesus

432 St. Patrick brings Christianity to Ireland

451 Council of Chalcedon

484 St. Brendan born

One of the famous beehive cells attributed to St. Brendan on Eileach an Naoimh

521 St. Columba is born

525 Dionysius Exiguus publishes the Easter Table

529-534 Justinian I publishes the Code of Civil Law

532 Nika Riots in Constantinople

533 Byzantines retake North Africa from the Vandals

542 The beginning of the plague in Europe

553 Second Council of Constantinople

563 St. Columba arrived in Hi, on Pentecost eve

563 St. Odhran dies, 27th of October

570 Muhammad is born

572 Connal, King of the Scots, who gave Hi to Columba, died

574 The great council of Drimkeat was held

577 St. Brendan dies

581 Sui Dynasty in China begins

583 Brude, son of Maolchan, King of the Picts, died

590 Gregory the Great becomes Pope

597 St. Columba, the Apostle of Albin, died 9th June

600 St. Baithen, son of Brendan, Abbot of Hi, died
Teotihuacan civilization is destroyed, Tikal is now largest Mesoamerican city-state

601 St. Laisran, son of Ferdach, Abbot of Hi, died

602-629 Last great Roman-Persian War is fought

618 Tang Dynasty in China begins

622 St. Fergna, surnamed the Briton, Abbot of Hi, died

624 St. Adomnan born

627 Battle of Nineveh, Byzantines, under Heraclius, crush the Persians

635 St. Aidan (Mac Libher) and others, set out for England from Iona, at the desire of King Oswald, to convert his people to Christianity

638 Jerusalem is captured by the Muslim army

643 Arab army takes Alexandria

645 Soga clan falls in Japan

650 Slav occupation of the Balkans complete

651 St. Segin, son of Fiachri, Abbot of Hi, died

651 St. Aidan, Bishop or Abbot of Lindisfarne in England, died. A number of his successors, such as Cellach, Fintan, Dima, Colman, etc. were also from Hi

654 St. Suibhne, son of Curtre, Abbot of Hi, died

660 St. Colman became Abbot of Hi, but soon after went to be Abbot of Lindisfarne, which he resigned in 664 and returned to Hi, after which he went to Ireland and built the monasteries of Innse-bosionn and Magheo

663 Synod of Whitby, Celtic Christanity is trampled by Roman Christianity in England

668 St. Cumin (Fionn) Abbot of Hi, the biographer of Columba, died
End of the Three Kingdoms period in Korea

672 Venerable Bede is born

674-678 First Arab siege of Constantinople broken, Islamic conquest of Europe adverted

677 St. Failbhe, Abbot of Hi, died

680 Third Council of Constantinople

684 St. Adomnan, Abbot of Hi, goes to reclaim from the Anglo-Saxons some captives and plunder; was honorably received and obtained all he wanted

685 Battle of Dun Nechtain, Picts defeat the Northumbrians

686 St. Adomnan, on a second embassy, got 60 captives restored from the Saxons to Ireland

695 St. Adomnan holds a Synod in Ireland; the acts of which are called "The Cannons of Adomnan"

698 Arab army takes Carthage

703 St. Adomnan, Abbot of Hi, and biographer of Columba, died

708 St. Conamhal, or Conain, son of Failbhe, Abbot of Hi, died

710 St. Caide, or Caidan, Abbot of Hi, died

711 Umayyad conquest of Hispania, begins Iberian Muslim rule until 15th century

713 St. Dorbhen Fada, Abbot of Hi, died

714 St. Faolchuo, son of Dorbhen Mac Teinne, made Abbot of Hi

714 The family of Hi (monks) expelled beyond Drimalbin, by Nectan King of the Picts

716 St. Duncha (or Duncan), son of Cinnsaola, Abbot of Hi, died, and Faolchiuo, who had resigned his office to him, again resumes it

718 Second Arab attack on Constantinople ends in failure

720 St. Faolchuo, son of Dorben, Abbot of Hi, died; the Annals of Ulster place his death in 723 and call him Faolan; which is the name retained by some of our old parishes

725 St. Killean, or Cillian, surnamed Fada, Abbot of Hi, died

726 Iconoclast movement begins in Byzantine Empire

729 St. Egbert, who had remained 13 years in Hi, died

735 Death of Bede

744 Many of the people of Hi perished in a great storm

747 St. Killean, surnamed Droicheach, Abbot of Hi, died (Annals of Ulster 751)

754 St. Failbhe II, Abbot of Hi, died

762 St. Slebhen, son of Conghal, Abbot of Hi, died

765 Beatus Nial, surnamed Frasach, King of Ireland (who abdicated

his kingdom and had been for eight years on Hi) died

767 St. Suibhne II Abbot of Hi, died (Annals of Ulster say 771)

768 The start of Charlemagne's reign

777 St. Muredhach (or Murdoch) son of Huagal, Prior of Hi, died

786 Beatus Artgal Mac Catheld, King of Connaught, who had abdicated, died in pilgrimage in Hi, in the eight year of his pilgrimage

787 Second Council of Nicea

793 Devastation of the isles by foreigners, Lindisfarne in particular, Viking Age begins

794 Heian period in Japan

795 City of Machu Picchu flourishes in Peru

797 St. Bresal, son of Seigen, Abbot of Hi for 30 years, died
St. Conmhal, Abbot of Hi, died

797 Hi burnt by foreign pirates

800 Charlemagne crowned Holy Roman Emperor
Gunpowder is invented

801 Hi again burnt by pirates, and many of the family destroyed in the flames

805 Of the family in Hi, 68 killed by foreigners (Ed. Note-Bay of Martyrs earned the name from this incident)

Modern day Iona, ancient and alive

810 St. Kellach, son of Conghad, Abbot of Hi, died

814 Charlemagne dies

815 Constantin, King of the Picts, builds the church of Dunkeld

816 St. Dermit, Abbot of Hi, goes to Albin with Columba's coffer or box

823 St. Blamhac, son of Flanni, Abbot of Hi, crowned with martyrdom, being slain by the Nortmans (Norwegians) and Danes (Ed. Note-For refusal to divulge to the Vikings the location of Columba's relics and treasures, he was dismembered on the very step of the holy altar)

827 Ungust II, King of the Picts, founded Kilrimont (St. Andrew's) Muslims invade Sicily

843 Kenneth Mac Alpin, after his conquest of the Picts, removes from the west to the east coast, creates the Kingdom of Alba

848 Jurastach, Abbot of Hi, goes to Ireland with Columkille's sacred things

849 Kenneth (III) transported the relics of Columba to his new church

852 Aulay, King of Lochlin, came to Ireland, and laid it under tribute

853 The Corab (successor or representative) of Columkille, a wise and excellent man, martyred among the Saxons

855 Russian nation founded by Vikings under Prince Rurik, Novgorod is made capital

863 St. Cellach, son of Ailid, Abbot of Hi, die in the land of the Cruthens (Picts)

864 Tuahal, Mac Artgusa, Abbot of Fortren, and Abbot of Dun-Caillen (Dunkeld) died

866 Fujiwara period in Japan
The Great Viking Army arrives in England

868 Earliest known printed book in China with a written date

871 Alfred the Great assumes the throne, uniting England

874 Iceland is settled by the Norse

875 St. Columba's box is carried to Ireland, lest it should fall into the hands of the Danes

877 Beatus Ferach Mac Cormaic, Abbot of Hi, died
(Annals of Ulster say in 879)

882 Kievan Rus is established

885 Arrival of SS. Cyril and Methodius in Bulgaria
　　Vikings attack Paris

890 St. Andrew's, about this time, made independent of Iona by King Grig

900 Lowland Maya cities in the south collapse, Maya in Yucatan still thrives

907 The Five Dynasties and Ten Kingdoms period in China commences

911 Viking Rollo and his tribe settle in what is today Normandy

927 Recognition of the Bulgarian Patriarchate, the first independent national church in Europe

935 St. Aonghus, son of Murchartach, co-adjustor of the Abbot of Hi, died

937 Dubharb, Coarb of Colum-kille and Adomnan, rested in peace

938 Battle of Bach Dang, marks the independence of Vietnam after 1000 years as a Chinese colony

945 St. Caoinchomrach, Abbot of Hi, died

958 Dubhdhunin, Coarb of Columkill, died

960 Mieszko, Duke of Polans, founds the Polish state

964 St. Fingin, Bishop of Hi, died

978 St. Mugron, Bishop, scribe, and notable teacher, surnamed Nantri-rann, Coarb of Columkill in Ireland and Scotland, died

979 Amhlua (or Aulay), son of Sitric, prince of the Nortmans, after his defeat in the battle Temora, took refuge in Hi, where he died

982 Eric the Red establishes a colony in Greenland

985 The island of Hi pillaged on Christmas Eve by the Nortmans, who killed the abbot and 15 of the learned of the church

988 Volodymyr I of Kiev embraces Christianity, it becomes the national religion

997 Patrick, Coarb of Columkill, died

988 Duncha, Coarb of Columkill, died

1000 Classic Pueblo period of Anasazi culture
Scandinavia converts to Christianity

1001 Leif Ericson settles L'Anse aux Meadows in Canada, the first European in the Americas

1004 B. Maolbrighde Hua Remed, Abbot of Hi, died

1009 Martan Mac Cineadh, Coarb of Columkill, died

1010 Muredach, Coarb of SS. Columba and Adomnan, an eminent professor of theology at Ardmagh, died

1015 B. Flannai Abhra, Abbot of Hi, died

1016 Canute the Great becomes King of England, Danes rule the next 26 years

1021 The Tale of Genji, written by Murasaki Shikibu, considered the world's first novel

1025 The Canon of Medicine is written, the standard medical textbook used in Europe through the 18th century

1040 MacBeth murders Duncan, King of Scotland (MacBeth later buried on Iona)

1054 The Great Schism between the Eastern Orthodox and Western Roman Catholics

1057 Robhertach Mac Donnell, Coarb of Columkill, died

1066 William the Conqueror, Duke of Normandy, invades England and becomes King after the Battle of Hastings, ending Anglo-Saxon rule, Orthodox hierarchs replaced by those loyal to Rome

1070 B. Macbaithe, Abbot of Hi, died

1077 Tower of London begins construction

1093 Magnus, King of Norway, subjugates the Western isles

1095 Pope Urban orders the Crusades, the first of nine total, to capture the Holy Land and repel the Turks from the Byzantine Empire

1098 The Cistercian Order is founded, following the Rule of St. Benedict

1099 B. Duncha, son of Moenach, Abbot of Hi, died

1116 The Byzantine Army defeats the Turks at Philomelion

1117 University of Oxford is founded

1118 Knights Templar are founded to protect pilgrims en route to Jerusalem

1126 The first legate (John of Crema) comes to Scotland, which is the first trace of Papal power there

1135 The Anarchy begins in England

1150 Angkor Watt is completed

1152 The Synod of Kells-Mellifont establishes the diocesan system in Ireland, bringing the Irish Church into mainstream Catholicism

1154 King Henry II establishes Common Law

1163 The first cornerstone is set for Notre Dame in Paris

1166 Stefan Nemanja unites Serbian territories

1171 King Henry II asserts his supremacy at the Synod of Cashel, English occupation of Ireland begins

1174 King William I of Scotland captured in the Battle of Alnwick

1175 Buddhist sectarian movement in Japan begins

1185 The relics of St. Columba brought to Down by order of Jo. De Curci Windmills are first created

1187 Saladin recaptures Jerusalem

1188 B. Amblua Hua Doighre, a pilgrim in Hi, died in a venerable

Marjorie Kunch

old age

1189 Richard I ascends the throne in England

1199 St. Muireach Hua Baodain died in Hi

1203 Ceallach built a monastery in Hi, in opposition to the learned of the place; upon which the clergy of the north of Ireland held a meeting; after which they came to Hi and demolished the monastery of Ceallach

1204 The Sack of Constantinople

1206 Mongol Empire established by Genghis Khan

1219 Serbian Orthodox Church becomes autocephalous

1297 The Battle of Stirling Bridge in Scotland

1298 Marco Polo publishes his tales of China

1314 Robert the Bruce victorious at the Battle of Bannockburn

1325 Renaissance begins

1333 St. Gregory Palamas defends Orthodox practice of hesychast prayer

1381 The Bible is translated in English by John Wycliffe

KINGS CONTEMPORARY WITH ST. COLUMBA

Of the Scots: Conal I. begins to reign, 560, Aidan, 575

Picts: Brude II 557 and Garnat IV 587

Strathclyde: Morken, 557 and Roderk 587

Ireland: Dermit I. 544, Fergus and Donald I. 565, Amirach 566, Beothan and Eoghan 569, Ed (or Aodh) I. 572

The holy well of St. Columba, found on Eileach an Naoimh, Hebrides, known as Hinba in his day

(L-R) Fr. Augustine McBeth-first Orthodox chaplain to the 568 year old University of Glasgow, author Marjorie Kunch, authors and Kellbride Press founders Father Michael Wood and Sister Margaret Smythe-monastics of St. Bride Heritage on Holy Loch, taken at St. Gabriel Orthodox Chapel, Scotland

The end.
And Glory to God!

More Titles From Pascha Press

When My Baba Died

When My Yiayia Died

Activity Workbook for When My Baba/Yiayia Died

When Mama Had Cancer

Found on Barnes and Noble, Amazon, and www.paschapress.com

www.ingramcontent.com/pod-product-compliance
Lightning Source LLC
Chambersburg PA
CBHW070430010526
44118CB00014B/1973